CODES
and Secret Writing

JAMES N. MATHER
INVERCORRY,
14, ST. MARY'S RD.,
DUNDEE, SCOTLAND.

CODES
and Secret Writing

HERBERT S. ZIM

A Piccolo Book

PAN BOOKS LTD
LONDON

First published in Great Britain 1965 by
World's Work Ltd.
This edition published 1971 by Pan Books Ltd,
33 Tothill Street, London, S.W.1.

ISBN 0 330 02822 7

Made and printed in Great Britain by
Cox & Wyman Ltd, London, Reading and Fakenham

Contents

Foreword

I don't recall whether I was in the fourth grade or the fifth when I 'invented' my first code. But I clearly remember what happened when a long code message I had written to my pal in the first row was intercepted in transit. At 3 o'clock, instead of the dreaded hour after school, my teacher talked with both of us about codes and expressed interest and satisfaction in my 'invention'. Her praise was so encouraging that I was easily persuaded to pay a bit more attention to geography and use the before-lunch reading period as a time for writing and decoding messages.

More recently, in working with educational programmes, my appreciation of my former teacher's wisdom has grown. The study of codes and secret writing is fun – fascinating fun. But at the same time it calls for a knowledge of science and of the English language. It demands logical persistent thinking that is found in few school subjects outside mathematics. It demands concentration and hard work. Yet it has been my experience that everybody, young and old, who is interested enjoys every minute he gives this hobby and, incidentally, learns a good deal in the process. If I were a teacher of English, science, or mathematics, I'd take advantage of the interest and satisfying activities that codes and secret writing offer – and I know that many teachers already do.

Secret messages, however, are not a subject to be

studied formally, but an activity to try and enjoy with your friends.

In writing this book I had the expert assistance of Gilbert Saul, who spent many hours in the laboratory testing and checking materials for secret writing. Mr William G. Bryan, Editor of the American Cryptogram Association, gave his invaluable advice and suggestions on the code chapters. My thanks are due to both these men and to the many young people whose constant interest in codes and secret writing is the real reason why this book came into being.

HERBERT S. ZIM

Port Washington, NY

ONE

Codes and Ciphers

Let's begin this book with a secret message:

⌐ ⊓⊔⊢⊡ <⊔⊓ ⊡⌐⌐⊔⊔< ⌐⊔⊐⊐⊡ ⌐⊐⌐
⊡⊡⊔⊡⊡⌐ ⊽⊡⌐⌐⌐⊡⌐

If you can't read it right off, it's a good sign that you may profit from the chapters that follow. Perhaps this message is easier:

R SLKV BLF VMQLB XLWVH ZMW HVXIVG
DIRGRMT

At least the letters are familiar, although their arrangement doesn't make sense – yet. Here's another sample:

VUBCR LBHRA WBLPB QRFNA QFRPE RGJEV
GVATN

This is an interesting puzzle. All the words are five letters long, and who ever heard of that kind of a message? Here is one final sample:

Yes, this last message inside the box is code combined with secret writing. The *invisible* ink can only be read by those who know how to make it visible again. All the above messages say the same thing:

I HOPE YOU ENJOY CODES AND SECRET WRITING

That is my hope, of course, because dozens of people I know have had fun with codes. And so can you, if you wish. The more you know about codes, the more fun they are likely to be. This book will help you with methods of making codes and using invisible writing.

Each of the messages you have just seen is in a different type of code. All of them are simple and are easy to learn. The idea of this book is not to give you codes to copy, but to help you to invent your own codes – not one or two but, if you like, hundreds of different codes. If you wish, you can have a different code for each of your friends to use. How you use your knowledge of codes is, of course, up to you.

When it comes to secret writing, the idea is to show you how to produce invisible writing with simple chemicals you have at home or can buy in the chemists – and to show you how to make this writing visible again. You won't be promised hundreds of different ways to write in secret, but you will find enough to keep you busy for a long time, if you test and try each way for yourself.

Most people never suspect how often codes are used by other people around them. An advertisement in a newspaper may contain a secret message. An innocent letter may bear a very different message written between the lines in invisible ink. Codes are used in the Ministry of Defence to send commands and messages to important officers in the Army, Navy, and Air

Force. Ambassadors and diplomats of all countries send their confidential reports in code. Even the businessman, who wants to buy and sell goods in some distant place, sends his order by cable code to save time and money. Codes are more important in real life than most people realize.

But let's go back to the beginning. Codes cannot exist without writing, and writing certainly had a beginning. When? That we do not know. But records show that writing was invented well over six thousand years ago. In those ancient times there were many spoken languages, but very few were written. The art of writing was known only by rulers, priests, and by men called scribes, who had the job of keeping records and writing messages. In those days, when very few people could read and write, *all* written messages were as good as code. Neither the messenger, who carried the clay or wood tablet, nor his friends who examined it when he stopped on the way, could understand what the marks in it meant. Since the messages in those days were intended to be secret and not to be read by every slave and peasant, the alphabet was to all intents a code – and a very good one.

The alphabet is the key to our story. The word itself is nothing more than the first two letters of the Greek alphabet: *alpha* (A) and *beta* (B). It was quite an invention and one that went through many improvements till our present model appeared.

Not very many people use the alphabet directly. Keep in mind as you read these words that you are paying no attention at all to the letters of the alphabet. Instead, you grasp the idea of a whole word or group of words at once. So, although the words are made of letters, you do not think of the separate letters as much as you might suppose.

Nowadays, when so many people can read, it is hard to imagine our usual writing as anything secret. But since most of us know only one language, anything written in another language is, for us, in code. This becomes an important point when you begin to count up all the known languages. No one will venture an exact figure as to how many languages and dialects (local forms of a language) there are. To put the number down at one thousand is making a very low guess. Some languages, like English, are spoken by hundreds of millions of people. Millions more understand Russian, Spanish, Chinese, and Arabic. But there are also many dead languages, known only by a few scientists who have studied them. For example, there is *Carian* – the language of a people who seem to have moved from Crete to Asia Minor long ago. There is *Oscan*, a bit like Latin and a bit like Greek. Not many people could decipher a document in these languages or, for that matter, in *Geez*, *Vedic*, or *Coptic*. They would all make excellent codes, if you and your friends knew them. Latin is more widely known than other dead languages, but so few people know it well that it could often be used as a code.

It is reported that during the last war a number of Navajo Indians in the American Army made good use of their native language to pass commands at the Front. There was very little chance for the enemy to detect the meaning of their strange tongue. Have you ever heard of *Hupa*, *Yuki*, *Nootka*, *Keres*, *Mixtec*, *Otomi*, *Catawba*, or *Chincook*? All these are languages of the American Indians – and there are dozens more, equally strange. Every one of these would make an excellent code. But don't get alarmed. This book isn't going to teach *Moqui* or *Winnebago*. If you *did* have a message in one of these, or even in French or Spanish –

and had the proper dictionary – the key would be in your hand.

Here is a message again:

ESPERO QUE LE GUSTE CODIGOS Y
ESCRITURAS SECRETAS

If you recognize this as Spanish and can lay hands on a Spanish-English dictionary, you will soon discover this message means exactly the same as the messages on page 9. You might have more trouble with:

НАДЕЮСЬ ЧТО ВАМ ПОНРАВЯТСЯ КОДЕКС
И ТАЙНОЕ ПИСАНИЕ

But it still says:

I HOPE YOU ENJOY CODES AND SECRET WRITING

If you recognized that the language was Russian, not Greek, Ukrainian, or Slavonic, you could decipher the sentence with the help of a Russian-English dictionary.

Do you think this a bit far-fetched for the idea of codes? If so, you are wrong. The whole idea of translating from one language to another is exactly the code idea. The purpose is different, of course, for foreign languages are not usually used to conceal ideas but to make them available to more people the world over. However, this is the time and place to clear up the question of what codes really are. The reason an explanation is necessary is that almost everyone uses the word 'code' in a very loose way. The title of this book should not have been *Codes and Secret Writing*, but

Ciphers and Secret Writing. You will find a brief mention of codes here before you go on to ciphers – because you are really interested in ciphers, even if you say you are interested in codes.

'A code,' says my biggest dictionary, 'is a system of words or symbols used to represent words or phrases for brevity or secrecy.' Notice, this definition says nothing about an alphabet; only about words and phrases. Let's look at an example of a code to get a better idea of what one might be like.

Code Word	*Meaning*
APPLES	PLEASE MEET ON ARRIVAL
PLUMS	AWAIT FURTHER MESSAGE
PEACHES	CALL A MEETING IMMEDIATELY
EATING	WILL LEAVE BY FIRST PLANE
PICKING	WILL LEAVE BY EARLY TRAIN
WASHING	WILL NOT LEAVE FOR SOME TIME
FATHER	MARSHAL OF THE ROYAL AIR FORCE
UNCLE	ADMIRAL OF THE ROYAL NAVY
GRANDPA	THE GENERAL STAFF

You can see how easily code messages can be made. The innocent message, FATHER EATING APPLES, would have a very different meaning to someone who knew it was in code and who had the code book. It would mean: MARSHAL OF THE ROYAL AIR FORCE WILL LEAVE BY FIRST PLANE PLEASE MEET ON ARRIVAL.

The message could be altered a little by adding words that don't mean anything, but which would make the message look even more innocent; for example: GRANDPA AND UNCLE HENRY ARE WASHING THE PLUMS. MOTHER IS MAKING JAM. This message would still mean: THE GENERAL STAFF

AND ADMIRAL OF THE ROYAL NAVY WILL NOT
LEAVE FOR SOME TIME AWAIT FURTHER
MESSAGE.

Codes have two distinct uses, as our definition tells
us. The first is brevity or shortness. If you are sending
a cable message from London to Melbourne, at 12p a
word, the shorter your message, the better. So you can
agree with the person in Melbourne to use the Western
Union Code, the Marconi Code, or some other. The
code book which you use contains thousands of five-
letter 'words', each clearly different from any other
'word' in the code. Each of these 'words' will mean
some phrase or sentence from two to a dozen words or
more in length. The person in Melbourne, who receives your cable in code, refers to the code book and
quickly finds the meaning of the 'words' you have
sent. Thousands of such code messages are sent every
day and their use cuts down the cost of long-distance
communications.

If you desire secrecy as well as brevity, you will have
to make up your own code, instead of using the
Western Union's. If you make your own code, you
must make at least two copies. You will use one when
you *encode* the message, and the receiver will use the
other when he *decodes* the message. Each copy of the
code would have two parts. In the first part, for encoding, you list in alphabetical order the English
words and phrases you are going to use and the code
for them. For example:

AM FEELING FINE	ARTOG
ARE YOU COMING	BELOG
ASK HIM ABOUT IT	ALMER
ATTEMPT TO DO IT	BAROW
AWAIT MY ANSWER	ALSOR

The second part of the code – for decoding – is arranged in the reverse order, with the code words in alphabetical order. For example:

ALMER	ASK HIM ABOUT IT
ALSOR	AWAIT MY ANSWER
ARTOG	AM FEELING FINE
BAROW	ATTEMPT TO DO IT
BELOG	ARE YOU COMING

With a good code you can send messages back and forth, feeling certain that no outsider will understand them unless a copy of the code book falls into his hands. An expert can sometimes decode a message without a code book, but this is a difficult job. It is only possible when a number of messages have been intercepted and certain key code words are found repeated in them.

One of the places where secrecy and brevity are both desired is in messages sent by the armed forces of all nations. So it is not surprising that codes are used in the Army, Navy, and Air Force, especially when there is little chance of the code books falling into enemy hands. It would be unwise to carry code books in planes flying over foreign countries. No one ever does. In the Navy, the code books are kept in a safe in the Captain's quarters. These important books are bound in sheets of lead. If, in battle or in an accident, the ship is about to sink, it is the duty of the Commanding Officer to throw the code books overboard. Their lead covers will carry them safely to the bottom. If there is any reason for believing that a code book has fallen into enemy hands, or even if some unauthorized person has had a look at its contents, then a new and entirely different code is substituted and the old one is never used again.

Secret codes are used in peacetime as well as in war. Our Government uses code to send important messages to ambassadors and other high officials in foreign countries. Delegates to the United Nations or to important international conferences may need instructions from home. If the matter is one of importance, codes are used. In every case, however, these codes consist of a list of 'words' which stand for other words or phrases. Codes do not make direct use of the alphabet.

These are codes and they are certainly useful. But if you had to go about with a thick code book tucked under your arm to send a secret message, the process would be rather tiring, instead of the fun that secret messages can be. So instead of a code you usually want a *cipher*. In a cipher, each letter of the alphabet is represented by one or more different letters or by signs. Knowing a cipher, you can make up any message you wish without the help of a code book. You can encipher the message any time or place and your partner can decipher the message right on the spot. You can keep most ciphers in your head and copy them down from memory, so there is no problem like losing a code book or forgetting it just when you need it most.

This great advantage of ciphers is also a disadvantage. If you should learn that the code word JACKO means I'LL SEE YOU TOMORROW, you know that one fact and no more. You do not know what JACET or JACOR or JOCKA means. They might mean anything at all. But if you should learn five key letters in a *cipher*, you would have little difficulty in figuring out what the other letters in a message might be. The five letters would enable you to 'break' the whole cipher and learn the rest of it in a short time. While a cipher may be more convenient to use, more practical, and much more fun, it is more easily broken than a code.

Much of this book will be devoted to different types of ciphers: how to make and use them. You will find some help in learning how to 'break' a cipher, but you might as well know right now that breaking a cipher is a slow and painstaking task that will call for all your skill and patience.

You will see the difference between codes and ciphers, but you can leave that difference to the experts. If you want to keep talking about codes, when you mean ciphers (as most people do), that is all right. This book will join you in using the more common, though less correct word. So let's go on to the easiest kinds of codes (or ciphers) and see what they are like.

TWO

The First and Simplest Codes

When people invent codes of their own, nearly all of them resemble the kinds of codes used hundreds of years ago before efforts to make codes scientifically really got under way.

These codes are based on the idea of using a single distinct *symbol* for each letter of the alphabet. And since each letter of the alphabet is itself a symbol, these codes do no more than substitute one alphabet for another. The symbols used long ago were more complicated than those we use today, but the idea was roughly the same. Some samples will make clear the simple way these codes were made and used. The first is a code (really a cipher) based on old signs used by alchemists and scholars in the Middle Ages. Here is part of it:

A	☉	F	☿
B	♃	G	♀
C	♄	H	♂
D	♆	I	☿
E	♅		

In this odd code, the name of this book would be:

ﾚﾊﾟﾖﾊﾟﾚﾟ   ⊙ﾚﾟ   ﾚﾟﾞﾊﾟﾞﾊ   ﾞﾊﾟﾞﾊﾟﾚﾟ

It certainly looks mysterious. But if you tried to use the code, you would find it difficult because the symbols are so hard to make and remember. Compare this code with the one that follows. This code was 'invented' by Harold, a junior schoolboy – and it's not a bad invention, at that.

A	▭	J	△	S	│
B	▣	K	▽	T	▯
C	▭▭	L	▿	U	▯
D	▤	M	▽	V	▦
E	▦	N	○	W	ﬣ
F	◹	O	⊖	X	✕
G	◺	P	⏀	Y	⌐
H	△	Q	⊕	Z	⊔
I	▲	R	⊙		

The Ministry of Defence will not want to adopt Harold's code, but it's interesting nevertheless. Notice that Harold used simple shapes and lines. Some of the code letters, like I and L, are very similar and might easily be confused. Such a mistake might spoil your chances of deciphering the message. This kind of code with an *invented alphabet* is easy to devise. You can make one yourself in just a few minutes. Here is one turned out on the typewriter, using only the keys with punctuation and other signs:

A	$	J	:	S	⧧
B	&	K	?	T	⧧
C	%	L	"	U	;
D	&	M	"	V	∴
E	'	N	-	W	/
F	(	O	±	X	/-/
G	)	P	@	Y	∴
H	+	Q	//	Z	-/-
I	@	R	⫽		

These codes all have one very serious drawback. You must remember each peculiar code letter or carry a copy of the code with you. If the symbols are complicated, the code is hard to use and errors may be made. Since speed and accuracy in encoding and decoding are very important, you can see why little attention (with one important exception) is given to invented alphabet codes these days.

It is worthwhile to think about invented alphabet codes a little longer, however, because there is a solution to the problem of remembering and using them. That solution is to develop some kind of *system* in the code. A system will help you to remember the code and will give you a clue as to what letters come next.

The very simplest kind of invented alphabet code, with an almost perfect system for remembering it, uses *numbers* for letters. It is an easy code to recognize, but it illustrates the idea exactly.

A	1	J	10	S	19
B	2	K	11	T	20
C	3	L	12	U	21
D	4	M	13	V	22
E	5	N	14	W	23
F	6	O	15	X	24
G	7	P	16	Y	25
H	8	Q	17	Z	26
I	9	R	18		

The nice thing about this code is that you can make a copy of it at a moment's notice. If you don't remember that O is 15 and W is 23, write down the alphabet and number the letters from 1 to 26. In using the code it may be wise to put a dash between letters. Otherwise U, which is 21, may be confused with BA, 2 and 1. With a number code the title of this book reads:

3–15–4–5–19   1–14–4   19–5–3–18–5–20
23–18–9–20–9–14–7

Once you start using this code it will become surprisingly easy. Before you know it, reading and writing messages will be possible with scarcely a glance at a copy of the written code. With just a few days' real practice for half an hour a day, you will be able to read messages in this code without the help of any written copy.

This brings us to a very important part of this book. Knowing *about* a code is one thing. *Knowing* a code is quite something else. Knowing a code requires practice, hours of it. There is no escape from it. Besides, the practice can be fun. It is nothing more than using the code, and that is what codes are for. After you have encoded and decoded a good many messages you will feel at home with the code and will be able to use it rapidly and with very few mistakes.

You can practise either by yourself or with a friend. Encode a message for your friend to decode. He can do the same for you. Have races to see how many words you can encode or decode in three or five minutes. For such a race, count every five letters as a 'word'. Add up the total number of letters in the message and divide by five to get the number of 'words'. In scoring, subtract three 'words' for every mistake. Accuracy is important. Mistakes are costly.

This book can help you with practice, but only to a small extent. For each type of code you will find a few practice exercises in encoding and decoding. After you have done them, make up messages of your own. The solutions to the practice exercises are given in the back of the book.

When you work with codes, accuracy is most important; speed comes next. Sloppy work spoils both. You must take enough time to do the job correctly. First, when you start to practise, you need some simple equipment. The best paper to get, is paper ruled in ¼-inch squares (¼-inch graph paper). If you can't get that, any ruled paper will do. You should have some sharp pencils with medium-hard lead. When you write, use only capital letters. Print each one large and clearly. Use all the space you need. Five words to a line are enough. To encode a message, first copy it on your paper in capital letters, five words to the line. If more than one line is needed, leave four lines before you continue. Then start at the beginning and write each code letter directly beneath each letter in the message. After you have completely encoded the message, it is good practice to break it up into 'words' that are five letters long. This destroys the clue that someone might get from the length of the words. If the last word has less than five letters, add meaningless letters (called *nulls*) to fill up the space.

Here is how a short message might be encoded:

```
M E E T    M E  A T    T H E
13-5-5-20  13-5  1-20  20-8-5

D R I N K I N G  F O U N T A I N
4-18-9-14-11-9-14-7  6-15-21-14-20-1-9-14

           A T    T W O
           1-20   20-23-15

13-5-5-20-13  5-1-20-20-8  5-4-18-9-14
11-9-14-7-6   15-21-14-20-1  9-14-1-20-20
           23-15-1-2-3
```

The final 1-2-3 (ABC) are nulls to fill in the space. When finished, copy the message on another sheet. Check the message against your worksheet to be sure there are no errors and then, of course, destroy the worksheet which would give your code away completely.

To decode a message, reverse the process. Copy the message on to squared or ruled paper, five 'words' to the line with four spaces between the lines. Then, using your code or memory, decode and write the message letters directly below. When the message is decoded, break up the five-letter 'words' into correct English. Here is an example, a reply to the last message:

```
19-15-18-18-25  2-21-20-9-23  9-12-12-2-5
S  O  R  R  Y   B  U  T  I  W   I  L  L  B E

20-5-14-13-9  14-21-20-5-19  12-1-20-5-1
T  E  N  M  I  N  U  T  E  S  L  A  T  E A
```

SORRY BUT I WILL BE TEN MINUTES LATE

(The A at the end is a null)

Now that you have an idea how to practise, turn
back to the number code and practise it, if you wish.
Here are three messages to encode and three to
decode. The solutions will be found in the back of
the book.

1. BE CAREFUL THE ROYAL TREASURER IS
   YOUR ENEMY
2. FOLLOW HIM CLOSELY AND REPORT WHAT
   HE DOES AGENT TWO J
3. A CODE IS LIKE A NEW LANGUAGE YOU
   MUST PRACTISE IF YOU WANT TO KNOW
   IT

Try to decode these:

4. 14–15–3–12–21 2–13–5–5–20 9–14–7–20–15
   13–15–18–18–15 23–1–2–3–4
5. 3–15–4–5–23 15–18–11–18–5 17–21–9–18–5
   19–3–15–14–19 20–1–14–20–16
   18–1–3–20–9 3–5–1–2–3
6. 2–5–3–1–18 5–6–21–12–25 15–21–1–18–5
   2–5–9–14–7 6–15–12–12–15 23–5–4–2–25
   5–14–5–13–25 1–7–5–14–20
   19–23–24–25–26

This number code has one weakness which everyone is sure to see. The code is too easy. Anyone could
guess what the numbers stand for. If they found the
message they could quickly break the number code
and figure out what you are planning to do. However,
something can be done to remedy this situation. You
can, for example, use only the odd numbers: 1, 3, 5, 7,

9, etc. There is no particular reason for beginning with 1. Start your code with 3. A is 3; B, 4; C, 5; and so on. Or use the numbers in reverse, so that A is 26; B, 25; and, finally, Z will be 1. You can start also at any number greater than 26 and work backwards and, if you give the matter some thought, you will find many more possibilities. These codes can be broken too, but not quite as easily as the first one.

Another simple code which substitutes numbers for letters is made by building a square of 25 boxes into which the alphabet almost fits. The 26 letters of the alphabet can be fitted into 25 squares because some are used less frequently, and two such letters can be put together. When decoding, the other letters in the word will show which of the two letters to choose. Letters often put together are I and J; Q and R; W and X. In this example I and J are put together. The square with the alphabet in place looks like this:

	1	2	3	4	5
1	A	B	C	D	E
2	F	G	H	I/J	K
3	L	M	N	O	P
4	Q	R	S	T	U
5	V	W	X	Y	Z

With this system, the code number for A is 11 because it is in the first row, first column; for H, 23 (row 2, column 3); and for M, 32. The row and column number identifies each letter. The code is a bit clumsy but it has been used with success. Here is a hidden message disguised as a grocery order.

Joseph Bulochi & Sons, Grocers
48 Liberty Street

Dear Sirs,

Please accept my order for the following and deliver at once:

43 tins best sardines	@	1/5
33 boxes soap flakes	@	1/4
23 large boxes dates	@	1/5
31 large tins peaches	@	3/5

Yours very truly,

Can you find the message hidden in this simple 'order' to the grocer?

This isn't all there is to invented alphabet codes. There are still other ways to make them and still other types which include our most important, though not our most secret, codes.

To repeat that all codes mentioned so far involve writing, is only to recall something too easily forgotten. *A written message has to be delivered.* One person must get the message to another. People have carried messages ever since they learned how to write. They used horses, camels, boats, and trains to help them. Messages were carried faster and faster, but never fast enough. About two hundred years ago a system of *visual* signalling was invented to send messages as fast and as far as the eye could see.

The heart of this system was a code with an invented alphabet. Two brightly painted boards were attached to a tall pole so that each could swing in a circle – something like your two arms. Each position of these boards represented a different letter of the alphabet. Both held horizontally, like your arms straight out to the sides, signalled R. This *semaphore*, set up on a hilltop, could be read miles away by a man with a telescope. He copied down the message and then sent it out over *his* semaphore for the next station to copy. Lanterns attached to the semaphore arms made it possible to send messages at night. A message was relayed from station to station much faster than a man could ride or carry it.

The semaphore code can be used with flags. Scouts often learn to use it. Semaphore can be used as a written code, too. Here it is:

For many years the semaphore system helped speed messages over Europe. Then, a bit over a century ago, our knowledge of electricity reached a point where scientists became convinced that it was possible to send messages at the speed of an electric current: 186,000 miles per second. It was Samuel Morse who made this idea workable when he built his first tele-graph in 1844. But with the telegraph, Morse had to invent a code. The semaphore was useless. The only thing that would travel through the electric wire was an electric current, so Morse built his code on the idea of turning the current on and off. Both semaphore and Morse codes use invented alphabets.

When the current ran through the wire for a very short time, it produced a short click in the telegraph which was written as a dot. A longer flow of current produced a long click – a dash. The combinations of dots and dashes make up the Morse Code. This code is used for radio as well as for the telegraph. Over the radio, the dot sounds like 'dit' and the dash sounds like 'dah'; so the radio man speaks of A as 'dit, dah',

A	·—	J	·———	S	···
B	—···	K	—·—	T	—
C	—·—·	L	·—··	U	··—
D	—··	M	——	V	···—
E	·	N	—·	W	·——
F	··—·	O	———	X	—··—
G	——·	P	·——·	Y	—·——
H	····	Q	——·—	Z	——··
I	··	R	·—·		

instead of 'dot, dash'. Of course, Morse Code can be written, too. It is certainly one of the most useful codes. You can use Morse Code with telegraph, radio, whistle, bell, flag, or in writing. The Morse Code is illustrated on page 29.

For practice, here are three riddles to encode:

1. WHEN IS A PIG LIKE INK
2. WHEN IS A PIECE OF WOOD LIKE A QUEEN
3. WHAT IS THE DIFFERENCE BETWEEN A
   JEWELLER AND A JAILER

The answers, even if you have guessed them, are here in code. Decode them for practice:

These are the codes, secret and otherwise, built on the idea of using some number, sign, or mark for each letter of the alphabet. Most other written codes use another system – not much harder to use and often much harder to break.

THREE

Position Codes

Anyone can invent codes using his own alphabet. There is no limit to the number if you use your imagination. But the system must be easy to remember, accurate and fast, if it is to be useful. Such codes are not easy to devise. However, we have just begun to explore and there are more kinds of codes to discover. One of them is a special form of an invented alphabet. It is a simple code. Yet it is not quite as easy to break as one which merely substitutes numbers for letters. In this new code it is *position* that counts. The idea of position is going to lead us into a whole new group of codes that you are sure to enjoy. A code where the position of a line or of a dot stands for a letter is a good one. The first example isn't a position code entirely, but it will give you the idea.

Start out by drawing two vertical lines and two horizontal lines across them, just as though you were

```
    A │ B │ C
  ────┼───┼────
    D │ E │ F
  ────┼───┼────
    G │ H │ I
```

playing noughts and crosses. If you fill the alphabet in the spaces, you will find you have room for nine letters.

A, for example, is ⌐; B, ⊔; C, ⌐. The letter E, ☐, is the only one completely enclosed. The code is easy to use.

HEAD is encoded as ⌐ ☐ ⌐ ⌐.

But this takes care of only nine letters. What about the rest? As soon as more lines are used you duplicate the pattern. One solution that makes a good and complete code is this one:

The use of dots makes it possible to use the same diagram pattern more than once. The alphabet is completely covered and the code works. The diagrams are so easy to memorize that once seen, the code can be copied down from memory and so you can have it ready for use in just a few seconds. This well-known code is called the Masonic cipher. During the American Civil War it was used by Northern prisoners in Confederate prisons to communicate with friends on the outside. All that is now needed is some practice with it. Try to encode the following messages:

1. WHAT IS THE ANSWER TO THE THIRD PROBLEM

2. HAVE YOU DONE YOUR HOMEWORK

3. DO YOU THINK THE QUIZ WILL BE HARD

These are messages to decode:

⌐⅂⅃⅃⅂ >⅃⅃∨⅂ ⊓⊏⅃⅃⊏ ∨⊏⊏⊏>

⅃⊏⊏<⅃ ⊓⅂⅃⌐⅃ ⅂⅃⅃⊓⊓ ⊏⅂⅃∧⊏ ⅃⅃⊏⊏⌐ ⅃⅃<⊓∧

⅂⊓⌐⊏∟ ⅃⊏⊏⊏⌐ ⅃⅃⅃<⊐ ⊏⅂⅃⅃⅃ ⅃<⊏⅃⊏ ⊏∟⊓⅃⅃ <⅃⅃<⊏

This code can be made with just the single pattern used for the first nine letters. To do this, *three* letters are put in each compartment, **ABC** in the first, **DEF** in the second, and so forth. A may be represented by ⅃, B by ∵⅃, and C by ∴⅃. If dots are not used, you must figure out for yourself which of the three alphabet letters each sign stands for.

This code uses the fixed position of a letter in a special diagram. The key to the letter is usually the position of the open side of the figure. There is no other difference between ⅃, ⊐, ⊓ and ⊏. But dots are also used and dots and boxes together keep this code from being a real code of position. Such a code, using position only, is possible. It looks quite mysterious, too. See how the title of this book looks in a position code. (It is shown on page 33.)

'How does a code like this work? It's nothing but dots!' True enough. It's the position of each dot that counts. Here is how to use this code. Typewrite the alphabet on a card or sheet of heavy paper. Make two copies – one for encoding messages and one for decoding. Cut the paper with the alphabet on it so that it looks like this strip:

```
| A B C D E F G H I J K L M N O P Q R S T U V W X Y Z |
```

If you can't use a typewriter, print the alphabet, but be sure that your two copies take up exactly the same space. The distances between the letters should all be equal. To encode a message, draw a margin line along the left side of the paper and set the edge of the alphabet strip against it. Be sure the edge is always touching the margin. Let's encode the word FISH. When the strip is in place, put a distinct dot right under F. Move the strip down slightly till the dot you have just made is completely covered. Put a dot under I. Move the alphabet strip down till the I dot is covered and put a dot under S. Then down once more and put a dot under H. Remove the strips and you have the word FISH represented by four dots.

In using this position code, remember that the strip for decoding must be identical with the one used for encoding. Be sure the strip stays exactly on the edge or margin as you encode your message. If it slips to the left or right, errors will result. Finally, move the strip down a small but definite amount between letters. If two dots are on the same level, more errors will pile up.

To practise this code an alphabet strip is needed. But you can make your own quickly on a typewriter. If necessary, trace the typewritten alphabet here and use it in practice. The alphabet strip printed below is made with capital letters on an elite-size typewriter, the most common size. There is a single space between letters and the total alphabet from A to Z takes up exactly $4\frac{1}{4}$ inches. If you copy this, make your copy $4\frac{1}{4}$ inches, too.

```
A B C D E F G H I J K L M N O P Q R S T U V W X Y Z
```

Now make your strip and encode these messages:

1. THE EMPEROR CHARLEMAGNE USED SEVERAL SECRET ALPHABETS
2. SOME PEOPLE BELIEVE THE BIBLE CONTAINS SECRET HEBREW CODES
3. THE FIRST BOOK ON CODES WAS WRITTEN SEVEN YEARS AFTER AMERICA WAS DISCOVERED

Here is a message to be decoded. Use the line to the left as the margin against which to hold your alphabet strip. (Illustrated on page 36.)

The dots in the position code can be used as dots or they may be connected with lines in a design or picture. At the bottom of page 36 is something that looks like an odd picture. Try to decipher it with your strip. A 'dot' is a place where any two lines join. Can you make out the message?

Do you think a simple position code is too easy? Perhaps it is. If you feel that way, there are dozens of ways of changing it. In each case a different pattern

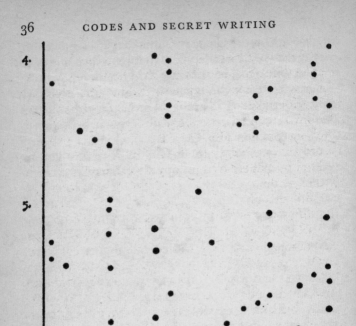

of dots will result. One way is to use the alphabet backwards, from Z to A. Another method is to start your alphabet with some other letter than A, with B or R or X. Continue right through to Z and then go

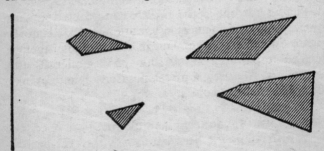

on through A, B, C till the alphabet is complete. A message encoded with an alphabet strip that begins at G cannot be decoded with the strip beginning with A.

A dot code can be made to use with an alphabet written vertically, as well as a horizontal one. And all the different arrangements of letters can be made to apply in this way also.

People are surprised to find a message can be written by the use of positions and without the use of letters. It does seem strange. Yet we use position with our alphabet all the time. The position of letters makes the difference between such words as PEA and APE or between MEAT and TEAM. Letters and their position both make our words what they are. Very few words are the same backwards and forwards, but here are some that are the same: ANNA, REPAPER, MADAM. People sometimes make a game of trying to write words or even sentences that have the same or some other meaning when read backwards. This means using the same letters and positions. Two well-known examples are: NAME NO ONE MAN and MADAM, I'M ADAM.

At any rate, in using our alphabet, both the letters and their positions are of equal importance in making words. Keep this fact in mind, for in all the codes from here on, the letters of our own alphabet will be used and the entire code will be based on changing their positions. When the letters are rearranged into the correct position, the message can be read, and not before.

The importance of position can be shown in a sample of the very simplest position code. Can you decipher this message?

EAR LYTOB EDEAR LYTOR ISEM AKE SAM ANHEAL THY WE ALTH YANDWI SE

Examine the message and you will see it is made of English letters, in exactly the same order as before the message was encoded. All that has been changed is the position of the break or space between words. The first word is EARLY but it is broken after EAR, and the LY is part of the next code word, LYTOB. The code message is nothing more than the old proverb:

EARLY TO BED, EARLY TO RISE, MAKES A
MAN HEALTHY, WEALTHY, AND WISE

Isn't it surprising how the change of position of just a few empty spaces can conceal an otherwise ordinary message?

The system of shifting the position of letters to hide the meaning of a message is called *transposition*. The codes in Chapter 2 are often known as *substitution* codes, because some sign or number is used as a substitute for a letter of the alphabet. Transposition codes are the type we will examine next. Both types of codes have been employed for many years. The transposition codes, which are used so much today, have been traced as far back as 500 BC. It is reported that the generals of the Spartan army sent messages to one another by using the simple trick of scrambling the letters in a message. The trick is such a good one, you may want to use it too.

This old code, called the Spartan scytale, requires some kind of a round rod. The Spartan general used his staff for the purpose. You may want to use a pencil or a piece of $\frac{1}{2}$-inch or 1-inch dowel stick, perhaps a foot or so in length. Whatever kind of stick you use, you have two of them the same size, because your partner cannot decode the message without one. The length of the stick isn't important. What counts is the diameter or thickness of the rod. Two sticks with the same diameter give us the two long cylinders that are needed to make the scytale work.

To use the scytale, cut a strip about a ½-inch wide from a fairly long piece of paper. Hold one end of the paper firmly near one end of the stick and spiral it around and around the rod. You can do this loosely and then tighten the spiral till the edges of the paper meet, forming a sort of spiral covering on your rod. After you have tried this several times, the scytale will wind naturally and smoothly. I've found that the paper may slip after it is wound, and so I use a bit of Scotch tape at each end to anchor it firmly in place. By now you are ready to write. Print your message down the length of the rod, one letter on each section of the spiralled paper. When the end is reached, turn the rod slightly and continue just as though you were writing on ordinary paper. Watch the spacing of the letters. Print in capitals as usual. When the message is complete, remove the paper strip and you will find your message reduced to a mysterious code. The letters running down the strip of paper seem to have no relation to the message you have written.

Your partner, when he receives the message, has only to spiral it around his rod and he can quickly read what you have written. If the message is wound around a rod that is thicker or thinner than the one you used, the letters will not fall into their correct place and the scytale will not reveal its message.

The scytale is no mystery. As the paper is wound around the rod, it passes the beginning point at regular intervals. When you write a message down the rod, the letters you write one after the other are actually put on the paper at regular intervals, with

ANCIENT SCYTALE

four or five or six other letters in between, depending on the number of rows in your message.

There are some advantages in using this kind of a mechanical code. You have nothing to remember, no signs or symbols. You write your message in everyday English. Once you have an idea about how many words you can put on your scytale, you don't even have to bother with a worksheet. As long as you have your rod, encoding and decoding are simple tasks, though carrying the stick around with you may be something of a nuisance.

The scytale has one difficulty. It's impractical to give you practice exercises. Make one for yourself and you will be surprised how well it works. The directions and the illustration will give you the start you need. After you have encoded half a dozen messages, using the scytale will be almost as easy as writing a letter.

The scytale means more than just a good code. It shows how messages can be scrambled according to a definite plan so that only those who know the plan can unscramble the message. The ways that messages can be scrambled are legion. In the next chapter are enough of them to lead you into modern scientific methods of making codes.

FOUR

Code Wheels

The scytale turns out to be an old but trustworthy device for changing the order of letters and moving them into positions which hide the meaning of a message. It is one example of a transposition code. Most transposition codes are more difficult. Substitution codes are generally easier, so the natural thing to do is to pay a bit more attention to these easier ones first.

Here is a simple substitution method, so simple it is hardly just to call it a code. Yet it is. It consists of nothing more than breaking up the English words. Another way consists of writing a message backwards; either the whole message is written backwards or it is written in the normal order with each word spelled backwards. For example:

JOHN IS GOING HOME EARLY TOMORROW – plain text

WORROMOT YLRAE EMOH GNIOG IS HNOJ – entire message backwards

NHOJ SI GNIOG EMOH YLRAE WORROMOT – words only backwards

If a message written entirely backwards is broken up into groups of five letters, it will certainly confuse anyone who does not know the secret. The message, completely encoded, looks something like this (note the two nulls):

WORRO MOTYL RAEEM OHGNI OGSIN HOJCX

These simple ways of moving the position of letters are quick and easy ways to conceal the meaning of a message. Once again, the meaning is hidden by changes of position.

Another simple code involves the alphabet rather than any message. Shifting the position of the letters of the alphabet in any way creates a simple code that substitutes one letter for another. If the alphabet is shifted one letter to the left, B takes the place of A, C takes the place of B, and so on down the line. The word CAB is encoded as DBC and is decoded merely by substituting the letter before each letter in the code. The shift can be two letters to the left, or three or four, or any number up to twenty-five. Shifts in the same way can be made to the right, and when these movements are exhausted more combinations can be made by reversing the alphabet and shifting again.

Should all these simple ways of transposing the alphabet seem confusing, a mechanical device will do the work for you and with very little effort on your part. The device is simple, too. The alphabet strip used for the dot code can be used again. Or make a strip by typing or printing the alphabet in capital letters with a space between. Then, on another strip, type or print two alphabets, one right after the other. Your final products should look like these:

ABCDEFGHIJKLMNOPQRSTUVWXYZ

ABCDEFGHIJKLMNOPQRSTUVWXYZABCDEFGHIJ ⎰etc.

By sliding the shorter strip along the edge of the longer one, you can set the alphabet with A over any other letter in the long strip. Then reading the code becomes nothing more than looking from one alphabet strip to the other. Set A over G, as shown above, and you have a code in which I becomes O, L is R, and R is X. Call this the 'G' code. All your partner has to do to decode a message is place A of his short strip over G on the long strip and the code letters on the *lower* strip will be directly under the message letters (or plain text, as the experts call it) on the upper row.

Changing codes is just as simple. You merely shift A over another letter, over C to use the 'C' code or over X for the 'X' code. With the two strips changing from code to code, encoding and decoding messages is no work at all. But there are drawbacks. These codes are the easiest to break. If you know these codes are being used, the meaning of just *one* letter will give the rest away. If you learn that U stands for O, you immediately know that V will stand for P, and W for Q. In a few minutes you will have the entire code – in this case the 'G' code – in which each letter is transposed to the seventh letter after. Since codes can be shifted quickly, use a different code for each day of the week. Perhaps 'M' on Mondays, 'T' on Tuesdays, and so forth. You may thus avoid having your code broken, even though it is easy to break.

In using the slide, the alphabet can be used forwards or backwards. By typing one alphabet strip from Z to A and the other from A to Z, you can get an entirely new set of codes which are just as easy to use. Call these codes 'reverse C' or 'reverse L', as the case may be. It is interesting to notice in these reverse codes that if I equals V, then V will also equal I and so on through the alphabet. When letters or numbers

line up this way, we say they are *reciprocals*. The
reverse codes are also easy to break. The reciprocals
help.

By now some practice is in order. Use the code
specified in each case. For example, use the 'G' code
for number 1. Encode these facts about codes:

1. (G code) JULIUS CAESAR USED CODES TO
   SEND MESSAGES BACK TO ROME
2. (R code) THE SEMAPHORE CODE IS WIDELY
   USED IN THE NAVY
3. (L code) MARCONI WHO INVENTED THE
   WIRELESS ALSO INVENTED AN EXCEL-
   LENT CODE TO GO WITH IT

Here are three messages to decode:

4. WIXYQ BYYFM QILEK OCWEF SQRST (U
   code)
5. MOOGD MOKUE QEEQZ FUMXU ZPQOA
   PUZSJ (M code)
6. SUDFW LFHDQ GPRUH SUDFW LFHPH
   DQVVX FFHVV ZLWKF RGHVA (D code)

Look at the device of two strips again, just to see
how it works. The double alphabet is needed because,
without it, the letters of your plain text or uncoded
alphabet would run off into space after Z. If you set
up a 'W' code, this would leave you with a good many
uncoded letters. The long double-alphabet strip is not
very convenient to carry around. Another code
invention, the *cipher wheel*, does away with the alphabet
strips. The cipher wheel merely bends the alphabet around in a circle till the Z and A meet. That takes
care of the problem of overlap and gives a fine,

pocket-sized code machine which works on exactly the same principle as the two alphabet strips. If you have made and used the strips, you will understand the cipher wheel much better. Be sure you try them before making a cipher wheel for yourself.

A cipher wheel is fun. You can't go wrong in making one and you will have a code machine in less than half an hour. For tools, get a pencil, a compass for drawing circles, and scissors. The materials you need: a sheet of fairly heavy cardboard, a pin, and a two-pronged paper fastener.

Set the points of your compass two inches apart. Draw a circle on the cardboard. This will give you a circle that is four inches across. Now set the compass points 1½ inches apart and draw another circle, which will be three inches across. Cut out both of them.

The next job may prove harder. It is to letter the alphabet around the edges of both circles, spacing it evenly. The quickest way to do this is to make a tracing of the long wedge shape printed on this page. Lay a piece of thin paper over the drawing and trace it. Then transfer your tracing to the cardboard and cut it out exactly. Be sure you copy the dot.

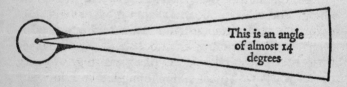

This is an angle of almost 14 degrees

This piece of cardboard will divide your 3- and 4-inch circles exactly 26 times and will help you place your alphabet neatly. Push a pin through the dot of the cardboard and right on through the centre of your circle. As you move the wedge around, draw lines to divide your circle. Do this to both circles. (Do them both at once, if you wish.) Then letter the alphabet around the outer edge of each circle, keeping the letters facing the centre.

When you have finished, push the paper fastener through the centre holes so that the circles can turn, and your cipher wheel is ready to use. You may prefer to cut a piece of plywood a bit larger than the 4-inch circle and fasten the circles down with a drawing-pin through their centres. Leave them free to turn and you are ready to go to work.

The outer circle should always be used as your plain text circle. To set up a 'D' code, place A on your outer circle over D on your inner circle and encode your message. To *decode* an 'S' code, place S in the *inner* circle under A of the outer circle and go right ahead. No practice is needed because the wheel works exactly the same way as the strips which you had a chance to try.

Finally, you may want to use the cipher wheel for reverse codes. To do that, make another *outer* circle and print the alphabet on it in reverse. You can work it in several ways. One is to remove your regular outer circle and put the reverse alphabet circle in its place. The other is to make two cipher wheels. Or, if you are very ingenious, you can work out a way to combine all these together into a single cipher wheel with three circles. If you feel like inventing, why not invent your own cipher wheel to handle both forward and reversed alphabets?

If the case of the cipher wheel were limited to these very simple alphabet shifts, it would hardly be worth a chapter even in a book for beginners such as this one. The simple substitution code made on a cipher

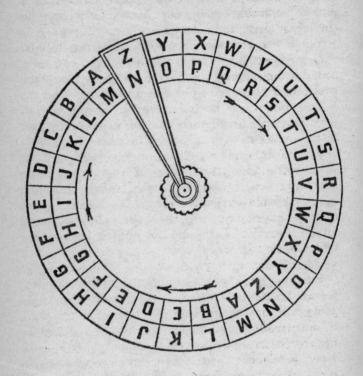

CODE WHEEL FOR REVERSE CODES

wheel hardly disguises a message. But if four, five, six, or even ten different codes were used in the same message, decoding by some outsider would become a very difficult task. Using many codes at once might be confusing, and also might lead to errors. This would certainly happen if it were not for the help of the cipher wheel. Here is the method for using several codes at once. It applies both to the ordinary cipher wheel and to one using reverse codes.

The core of the method is the use of a *keyword*, so we might call these *keyword codes*. Keywords are used in a number of ways. This is only one of them. The keyword can be any word or name, as long or as short as you wish. Only two things are important. The first is that no letter should be repeated in the keyword. *Keyword* would make a good keyword; no letters in it are duplicated. So would *island, brick, parchment, silver,* or *fish*. Second, the keyword should be an easy one to remember.

The choice of the keyword should not be made lightly, because each letter in the keyword stands for a different code. The keyword *cat* means that three codes are used: 'C' code, 'A' code, and 'T' code. The keyword *parchment* gives you nine codes. If your message is short, a short keyword will be more suitable. A longer, more important message might demand a longer keyword. If you remember the keyword and have your cipher wheel at hand, messages can be sent and read easily.

The explanation of how the keyword method works will not be complete till you have tried it out for yourself. So follow step by step, and do the work on your cipher wheel as you go.

Start with a very simple message: LEND ME A PEN. Send it with the keyword *cub*. First print the message out with several blank lines beneath it. Then, under the message, print the keyword over and over again till there is a keyword letter for every letter in the message. Your message now looks like this:

```
LEND   ME   A   PEN
CUBC   UB   C   UBC
```

With a longer message you might write *cub* twenty times or more. Don't be bothered if the keyword is not complete at the end. Now you are ready to encode. Since the first letter of your keyword is C you use the 'C' code by setting C on your *inner* cipher wheel under A on your *outer* cipher wheel. With your 'C' code you encode *every letter in your message that is on top of a C* and no others, as the example shows. In this example you encode L, D, A, and N in the 'C' code and write the code letters below. When you have finished, your message looks like this:

```
LEND   ME   A   PEN
CUBC   UB   C   UBC
N  F        C    P
```

Go through the message again, using the 'U' code, since U is the second letter of the keyword. Encode all the message letters which are above the U. These are E, M, and P. Write the code letters below and the code has now reached this stage:

```
LEND   ME   A   PEN
CUBC   UB   C   UBC
NY F   G    C   J P
```

Only three letters remain to be set up in the 'B' code, the final letter of the keyword. The letters to be encoded are N, E, and another E. Set B of the inner wheel under A of the outer wheel and go ahead. When finished, your message is encoded:

```
LEND   ME   A   PEN
CUBC   UB   C   UBC
NYOF   GF   C   JFP
```

Three distinct codes have gone into this message: 'C', 'U', and 'B' codes.

But the job is only half done. Messages have to be decoded. The process is exactly the reverse. Sticking to our example, we find ourselves with the message, NYOF GF C JFP. We remember that the keyword is *cub* and so we get to work. Write *cub* over and over again under the message just as before:

```
NYOF   GF   C   JFP
CUBC   UB   C   UBC
```

Again set up the 'C' code first. In decoding look for code letters in the *inner* ring to find the plain text message in the outer ring. With the 'C' code (C set under A), N on the inner wheel gives L outside. We go on, and look up F and C and P. Our message now stands:

```
NYOF   GF   C   JFP
CUBC   UB   C   UBC
L  D        A   N
```

Notice that we don't learn much about the message from the first code alone. Now we fill in with the 'U' code and decode Y, G, and J. We now have:

```
NYOF   GF   C   JFP
CUBC   UB   C   UBC
LE D        M   A P N
```

In the last lap we decode with the 'B' code to fill in the missing letters and read, LEND ME A PEN.

You may have noticed that the code message had three Fs in it. One F stood for a D; the other two stood for E. A message might have a word like 'beetle' containing three Es. With the keyword *roast*, the first E would encode as S; the second E would encode as E (in the 'A' code, there is no change) and the third E would end up as V. Pretty confusing to anyone who doesn't know the keyword!

All this is not very difficult, but to use this kind of code requires skill that can only come with practice. You may make mistakes at first. Check back and see how they happened. After your practice you will agree that the keyword codes are among the best to use.

For practice, encode the following messages with the following keywords:

1. THE CAVE IS MINED   Keyword *bet*
2. DO NOT TRUST SILAS JONES   Keyword *loaf*
3. ARE YOU INVITED TO THE
   PARTY   Keyword *candy*

Now decode these short messages:

4. JCGWL VAYIY PQEDC   Keyword *house*
5. PWWPG KMULS GOMXL
   LYVRS   Keyword *island*
6. KVEKX TCDWL RFEZT
   IRTGU ISACQ   Keyword *roast*

These substitution codes are about as difficult as any you may want to try, and this might be a good place to stop, except for one point that cannot be overlooked. These codes require the use of the cipher wheel. Any code that needs such help isn't the kind you can carry completely in your head, which is the best place to carry a code. So the remaining codes, though hardly ever more difficult, are codes that require nothing more than your remembering the system, and the system is nothing at all to remember!

FIVE

Multiplication Table Codes

Do you remember the multiplication tables? Of course, but what has that to do with codes? Multiplication tables, like 4×4 or 3×8, are the key to the excellent transposition codes you will find in this chapter. They can all be set up quickly without the aid of a code wheel and all are stickers to decipher without a key.

Before going into details, remember that in transposition codes the *system* is important, and we are back to transposition codes again. The system may be a very simple one as in this first example, a well-known code. People call it the Rail-Fence code, because the letters zigzag like an old rail fence when the message is encoded. With it you can encode a message as fast as you can write.

SEND US HELP AT NOON

Let's set this urgent message up in Rail-Fence code. Copy the message on your worksheet in *two* lines – the first letter of the message on the top line, the next letter on the line below, the third letter on the top line again, and so on. In a minute your message will look like this:

S N U H L A N O
E D S E P T O N

Now move the second line up to the end of the first and your message reads:

SNUHLANOEDSEPTON

This can be broken up into four 4-letter 'words' which encode the message as:

SNUH LANO EDSE PTON

If you want your message in standard 5-letter 'words' add any 4 letters as nulls before encoding. Let's add CIBD as nulls to the original message which now reads:

SEND US HELP AT NOON CIBD

Separate into two lines as before we get:

S N U H L A N O C B
E D S E P T O N I D

Moving the second line to the end of the first and breaking the text into 5-letter 'words' gives us the message completely encoded:

SNUHL ANOCB EDSEP TONID

Encoding with the Rail-Fence code is fast, once you've mastered its trick. Decoding is just as easy. Since writing the message on two lines actually divides the message in half, doing just that is the first step in decoding. Count the letters and divide the coded message in half.

SNUHLANOCB EDSEPTONID

Once this is done you can begin to read the message immediately, taking the first letter from the first half, then the first letter from the second half; next the second letter from the first half, and so on till the coded text is finished. Write the message down and it will end up as:

SENDUSHELPATNOONCIBD

which is the original message plus the four nulls.

The Rail-Fence code is an important step in understanding the multiplication table codes which follow. So practising this code is decidedly worthwhile. Encode the following facts about codes and ciphers in Rail-Fence code:

1. EDGAR ALLAN POE WAS AN EXPERT ON CODES AS WELL AS A WRITER
2. AN OFFICIAL AMERICAN CIPHER WAS SET UP AS THE CONSTITUTION WAS ADOPTED
3. THE UNION ARMY EASILY DECIPHERED MOST CONFEDERATE CODES DURING THE CIVIL WAR

Decode these messages from Rail-Fence:

4. RIFNE SHFSE TRNPS TOCDA ALECI TEATS TASOI INOEB
5. CDMCI EECPE ADEIH RESGS AILWY OEAHN SNIHR NDCPE MSAER PDYXZ
6. TETDO TEITR OTELH BTEEL MNSRN EATHJ HSUYF HHSOY FHAPA ERVAS AYTAG FCSIK

Now let's examine the Rail-Fence code more carefully and see how it works. By setting one letter on one line and the next on the line below, we are actually dividing the message up into a series of columns each two letters high. The 16-letter message becomes 8 columns of 2 letters each, and 8×2 gives 16. The columns are then read off *horizontally* to encode the message. Whatever the length of the message, it is always set in columns of two in the Rail-Fence code. The number of columns is always the length of the message divided by 2.

There are many other ways to divide up a message, using this same idea. Let's continue with our 16-letter example, SEND US HELP AT NOON. What two numbers multiplied together give 16? From the Rail-Fence code it's already clear that 8×2 is one answer and 2×8 is another. So is 4×4. In the Rail-Fence code we arranged the message in 8 columns of 2 letters each. We could also arrange the message in 2 columns of 8 letters each or in 4 columns of 4 letters each. The patterns would then look like these:

```
8×2                      2×8            4×4
S  N  U  H  L  A  N  O    S  L          S  U  L  N
E  D  S  E  P  T  O  N    E  P          E  S  P  O
                          N  A          N  H  A  O
                          D  T          D  E  T  N
                          U  N
                          S  O
                          H  O
                          E  N
```

In each case you can still read the message by reading down one column after another. To encode the messages all you do is to take the message off *horizontally*, and then break the message up into 4-letter 'words'. Here is how these messages would look:

8×2 SNUHLANOEDSEPTON

         or   SNUH   LANO   EDSE   PTON

2×8 SLEPNADTUNSOHOEN

         or   SLEP   NADT   UNSO   HOEN

4×4 SULNESPONHAODETN

         or   SULN   ESPO   NHAO   DETN

Messages can be encoded a number of different ways, depending on how many pairs of numbers can be multiplied together to give the number of letters in the message. A message of 80 letters can be encoded in these patterns:

$$2 \times 40 \quad 4 \times 20 \quad 8 \times 10 \quad 10 \times 8 \quad 20 \times 4 \quad 40 \times 2$$

Each of these six ways will give a differently encoded message, just as the three methods in the example just given produced three different code messages.

The person who is going to decode your message only needs to know the multiplication table key: 4×4 or 2×8 or whatever it is. This tells him the system used in transposing the message. Decoding is then an easy matter. If the key is 2×8, your friend knows that you have encoded a 16-word message ($2 \times 8 = 16$) by setting up 2 columns of 8 letters each. (We still have our sample in mind.) So he goes to work in *reverse* and breaks the coded message up into 8 groups of 2 letters each, to look like this:

SL   EP   NA   DT   UN   SO   HO   EN

He writes these groups in a column with SL at the top and continuing through to EN. This makes 2 columns of 8 letters each once more. When this is done, reading down the first column and then down the second gives the original message. If the key had been 4×4 the 16-letter message would be decoded by breaking it into 4 groups of 4 letters, setting these in columns, and reading down one after another to decipher the message.

One more message, a bit longer, will clinch our example and send us on to the next and final step:

WHAT IS THE ANSWER TO QUESTION FOUR

That might be an important message requiring careful concealment. The message has 29 letters and no two whole numbers multiplied together give 29. Add a single null to get a 30-letter message which can be set up with 5×6, 6×5, 10×3, 3×10, 15×2, or 2×15 as the key. Or add 3 nulls to make a 32-letter message which could be encoded 8×4, 16×2, 4×8, 2×16. Let's try a single null, E, and set up the message in 6×5 code. Here it is, broken into 6 groups of 5 letters.

WHATI STHEA NSWER TOQUE STION FOURE

Arranged in 6 columns we now get:

```
W  S  N  T  S  F
H  T  S  O  T  O
A  H  W  Q  I  U
T  E  E  U  O  R
I  A  R  E  N  E
```

Reading horizontally again, the message is now:

WSNTSFHTSOTOAHWQIUTEEUORIARENE

which, in 5-letter 'words', becomes:

WSNTS FHTSO TOAHW QIUTE EUORI ARENE

To decipher this urgent message, your friend, knowing the key is 6×5, breaks the message up into five *6-letter groups* and writes one group below the other. This duplicates the diagram above and the message becomes clear by reading down the columns or copying one column after another.

Now, once again, practice is in order. Put these three messages into code using the key that is given:

1. BRING THE PLANS TO THE OLD
   OAK   Key 4×6
2. TREASURE BURIED TEN PACES
   EAST OF RED ROCK   Key 5×7
3. WE ARE HAVING A SPECIAL
   MEETING IN THE CLUBHOUSE
   AFTER SCHOOL   Key 5×11

Now to reverse the process. Here are three code messages to decipher. Do them as fast as you can – so long as you remember that accuracy comes first. Time yourself and see if you improve, even though each message is harder than the last.

4. HMEII AIPNS VTOPN EHRAO
   SRTRW   Key 5×5
5. CTTEB OOEOA ANTAN ANCGT
   WTCBA   Key 8×3
6. CNTAU IROTI ITDSN PCNOE
   ASRES ARBTA TYVRC ACROO
   ODABC   Key 7×6

This is a bare introduction to a very complex group of codes, too complex to be treated in detail in this first book of codes and secret writing. Yet transposition codes are so important that we should move along just a bit further. Then the people who are good at codes of this kind will see the way to invent many others that are fine to use because they are so difficult to break.

The codes in this chapter have been made by arranging the message in one pattern and *transposing* it into another. The words have been set up in a vertical line and have been transposed into a horizontal one. There are other ways that a message can be transposed, all using the same principle. Each new way results in a new code, one that will be just as easy to use as those already described.

Instead of telling about each of these ways, they have been set up as two different kinds of examples: first, as the alphabet, using I for both I and J; and, second, in the form of a simple message BRING THE MONEY WITH THE PLANS.

Here is the first transposition, with the message arranged in vertical lines, letters moving forwards. It is the method we have just been using.

Vertical pattern, letters forwards

```
      A F L Q V              B T N T P
      B G M R W              R H E H L
      C H N S X              I E Y T A
      D I O T Y              N M W H N
      E K P U Z              G O I E S
```

AFLQV BGMRW CHNSX   BTNTP RHEHL IEYTA
      DIOTY EKPUZ   NMWHN GOIES

As the first new step, use the same plan with the letters arranged in columns from *right* to *left* instead of from left to right. In other words, set the columns up backwards:

Vertical pattern, letters backwards

```
      V Q L F A              P T N T B
      W R M G B              L H E H R
      X S N H C              A T Y E I
      Y T O I D              N H W M N
      Z U P K E              S E I O G
```

VQLFA WRMGB XSNHC   PTNTB LHEHR ATYEI
      YTOID ZUPKE   NHWMN SEIOG

Here is the same pattern again, but with the code in completely reversed order. See what this variation is like:

Vertical pattern, letters reversed

```
        Z U P K E              S E I O G
        Y T O I D              N H W M N
        X S N H C              A T Y E I
        W R M G B              L H E H R
        V Q L F A              P T N T B
ZUPKE YTOID XSNHC      SEIOG NHWMN ATYEI
    WRMGB VQLFA            LHEHR PTNTB
```

By moving backwards or in reverse, the letters and the word order in the code are rearranged, but the person who knows the key (in these cases 5 × 5 backwards and 5 × 5 reversed) can decode the message on sight. The next step is only slightly more difficult. Instead of setting up vertical columns, we work on a slant and put our message on a diagonal line. The example will make this clear. First follow the alphabet.

Diagonal pattern, letters forwards

```
        A B D G L              B R N H N
        C E H M Q              I G E E T
        F I N R U              T M Y H E
        K O S V X              O W T P A
        P T W Y Z              I H L N S
ABDGL CEHMQ FINRU      BRNHN IGEET TMYHE
    KOSVX PTWYZ            OWTPA IHLNS
```

The same diagonal pattern which gives such a very different code from the vertical column can also be used backwards. Here it is:

Diagonal pattern, letters backwards

```
    L G D B A              N H N R B
    Q M H E C              T E E G I
    U R N I  F             E H Y M T
    X V S O K              A P T W O
    Z Y W T P              S N L H I
LGDBA QMHEC URNIF    NHNRB TEEGI EHYMT
   XVSOK ZYWTP          APTWO SNLHI
```

The diagonal pattern can also be used in complete reverse:

Diagonal pattern, letters reversed

```
    Z Y W T P              S N L H I
    X V S  O K             A P T W O
    U R N I  F             E H Y M T
    Q M H E C              T E E G I
    L G D B A              N H N R B
ZYWTP XVSOK URNIF    SNLHI APTWO EHYMT
   QMHEC LGDBA          TEEGI NHNRB
```

A variation on this method of encoding moves *down* the first column but *up* the next. This is called an *alternate vertical* pattern and it is commonly used. The alphabet looks like this:

```
         A K L U V
         B I  M T W
         C H N S X
         D G O R Y
         E F P Q Z
    AKLUV BIMTW CHNSX DGORY EFPQZ
```

You can develop other types of alternate patterns, moving *up* the first column and *down* the next or using a horizontal pattern instead of the vertical.

Finally, to show what can be done with simple

transposition codes (yes, these are still simple) the code can be arranged in a spiral pattern. Here is the alphabet, spiral pattern with letters forwards:

```
A  B  C  D  E
Q  R  S  T  F
P  Y  Z  U  G
O  X  W  V  H
N  M  L  K  I
```

ABCDE QRSTF PYZUG OXWVH NMLKI

Work out for yourself what our code message would look like when encoded on a spiral pattern with the letters forwards. Then, if you are ambitious, try the spiral pattern with letters reversed. You can even work out more complicated alternating patterns if you use your imagination.

In the first transposition codes, the message was arranged in columns and encoded horizontally. That is still the simplest and easiest way to use these codes. If you are trying some more complex style, be sure your key indicates exactly how to decode. Messages of 16, 25, 36, or 49 letters are fine for practice, and if you use a few nulls the messages can be made this length. Otherwise, you should adapt your code to your message length. It hardly pays to use a spiral, backward transposition code for a three-word message.

One weakness in the transposition codes so far is the fact that the columns follow one another in some kind of regular order. These weaknesses can be overcome by a simple number key which is even easier to remember and which makes the code even harder to break. The method is so simple that it seems essential to include it.

Write the message in the usual way and decide on

a multiplication table pattern to fit it, perhaps 4 × 10 or 5 × 6 or 8 × 12. Arrange the message (with nulls if necessary) to fit the pattern in the usual way. Now instead of taking off the message in horizontal rows, stop and number each column from 1 up as far as you need to go. Your next step is to select a key number which has as many digits as you have columns, and in which no digit is repeated. If your code has 4 columns, you can choose 1492 or 1948 as key numbers. But you cannot use 1776 because it has two 7s. A 6-column code would require a key number like 158329 or 765234.

Now rearrange your key number so that you put the lowest digit over the first column, the next over the next, and so on. You end up with your key number arranged so that its lowest digit is on the left and the highest is on the right. Use zero as the highest. Here is how a 4-column code might look with the number 1492 as the key number:

        1 2 4 9 — key number rearranged
        1 2 3 4 — column numbers
        E R L S — first row of text

When this is done, arrange your key number back in the right order again, *but move each column as you change it*. In this case the first column stays the first. The third becomes the second. The fourth becomes the third and the second becomes the fourth. The rearranged key (1249) becomes 1492 again and the columns are no longer in their original order.

The rest is easy. Transpose your message into horizontal lines as before. Whoever knows the key number also knows how many columns to set up. An example will show the code in action.

PLEASE RETURN BY TRAIN

The message has 19 letters. So we add a null, X, to make it 20. This message can be set up as 4×5 which will permit us to use a date as a key number. Here is the code set up as 4×5 with one null. Let's use 1948 as the key number:

```
P E R R
L R N A
E E B I
A T Y N
S U T X
```

Now number the columns:	Put the key number over columns with lowest digit to left:	Rearrange columns so that key number is returned to correct order:
	1 4 8 9	1 9 4 8
1 2 3 4	1 2 3 4	1 4 2 3
P E R R	P E R R	P R E R
L R N A	L R N A	L A R N
E E B I	E E B I	E I E B
A T Y N	A T Y N	A N T Y
S U T X	S U T X	S X U T

Now set the message off in horizontal rows to give:

PRER LARN EIEB ANTY SXUT

And, if you wish, change it into 5-letter 'words';

PRERL ARNEI EBANT YSXUT

Your friend who gets the message knows that the key

is 1948. That tells him that the message is to be
arranged in 4 columns and in what order. So he copies
the message down as follows under the code number:

```
1 9 4 8
P R E R
L A R N
E I E B
A N T Y
S X U T
```

The next step is to arrange the key number in order
from the lowest digit to the highest, moving the
columns accordingly. This gives:

```
1 4 8 9
P E R R
L R N A
E E B I
A T Y N
S U T X
```

By reading down the columns, the message is immediately clear.

PLEASE RETURN BY TRAIN

This is the end of all the codes. So here is some final
practice. Encode the following messages:

1. DO NOT COME TO MEETING
   PLACE   Key 1864
2. ALL WORK WITH CODES
   REQUIRES PATIENCE   Key 54321
3. THE SCIENCE OF BREAKING
   CODES IS CALLED CRYPT-
   ANALYSIS   Key 51423

Decode these messages:

4. BSWIL TILOR NLOET
   FDEHL WTEOX   Key 1953
5. HMIIM EEELM LFNLY
   PRDCF WOSOR   Key 13524
6. ONLAT EOUTE FHCBL
   OATEO REMRE MDEAA
   NRHEA RKTYZ SKABC   Key May 23rd, 1948
                                     (23/5/1948)

With this introduction to codes and ciphers you
should be able to make all the codes you will ever
need. You can feel sure that only a person who has
had long experience with codes will be able to break
your messages, if you use codes like those in this
chapter. So now it's time to look at the task of breaking
codes. It will make you appreciate the codes you have
been using. Code breaking is not easy, patience is
needed, and under some circumstances even the experts fail. But the methods themselves are quite simple.
You will find them in the next chapter.

SIX

Breaking Secret Codes

The idea behind most codes is to send a message which can only be understood by the people who know the secret. For you and thousands of others sending secret messages may be fun. But there are times and places where secrecy is essential. In some Government business and during wars, secrecy is of utmost importance. Wars depend as much on secret codes and ciphers as on guns. If the secret codes used in warfare are broken, the cost may be very great. The stories of how enemies were thwarted and victories won because secret codes were broken are more thrilling than the stories of battles themselves. The wars between the code breakers and code makers pitted the skill, knowledge, patience, and sometimes luck of one side against the other.

This chapter is an introduction to the art and science of breaking codes. This science is called *cryptanalysis*, a word that means the analysis or taking apart of secret writings. The principles used in cryptanalysis are the same as those a detective employs in putting together the clues to a crime or those used by a scientist in searching out the clues to a secret of nature. In both cases clear, careful thinking is essential. Patience and persistence are as necessary as the paper and pencil with which the cryptanalyst works.

The clues used in breaking codes are the very words themselves. Messages may differ in length and meaning.

But no matter what they say, they all contain words. The clues in words are the main clues that you can use. There is one other source of clues: *some system* must have been used to transform a clear message in English, or any other language, into a secret one. The fact that there *was* a system for encoding the message provides another type of clue that helps to reveal the secret.

Cryptanalysis can be as exciting as football and as challenging as a chess game between experts. It is a hobby that many people find more interesting and difficult than most games of skill. But this type of code breaking requires years of study and practice. Since we are just beginning, we can only touch on the simplest methods. The purpose here is to show you how codes are broken and to give you simple tools for breaking them. But skill can only come from your own efforts.

For our work we can take it for granted that the hidden message is in English, and that it is made up of words we normally use in our everyday speech. If a message were made up of specially chosen words, such as those used by a chemist, doctor, or stockbroker, the task of breaking the codes would be greatly increased.

The very first step in breaking codes requires at least a passing familiarity with them. In deciding where and how to begin one must at least guess if one is dealing with a code or with a cipher (see Chapter 1). If the form of the message indicates that it is a true code and not a cipher, none of the methods in this chapter will be of much help. The breaking of a true code is very difficult because the clues that may be present within the words are lacking. Assuming that a cipher is used, the next step is to decide which of the two basic types has been employed, substitution or transposition. To make this decision some important facts about the English language must be known.

In the English language we use an alphabet of 26 letters. But the letters are not all used to the same extent. Some letters are rarely used at all. Others are so essential that it is hard to write a sentence without them. The letter E is used about two hundred times as often as the letter Z and about one hundred times as often as the letter J. S is used three times as much as G, and O is used three times as much as C. Many studies of the frequency of letters in the English language have been made. Samuel Morse made such a study when he made his Morse Code. Edgar Allan Poe did too. Dozens of other studies are all in reasonably close agreement. The printer who sets up type knows this fact about our alphabet and uses it every day. The case in which he keeps his type is divided up into compartments. The letters used most get the largest boxes and those that are easiest to reach.

The most common letter in the English language is E. The least common is Z. The list in order of use is as follows:

ETAONRISHDLFCMUGYPWBVKXJQZ

Some experts list Q before X, and L before D, but there is pretty close agreement on the first dozen letters and they are the important ones.

A, E, I, O, U, the vowels, make up 39% of all the letters used in the many messages studied. The five most common consonants, H, N, R, S, T, are used almost as much as the vowels – 33%. The first five letters on the list, E, T, A, O, N, make up 45% of the English language. And the first nine letters, E, T, A,

O, N, R, I, S, H, make up 70% of the letters which form the words on this page.

-	[ ]	æ	œ	( )	j				'	?	!	;	'	fl
& / fff	b	c	d		e	i		s	f	g				ff / fi
ffi / k	l	m	n		h	o	y	p	,	w				
x / z	v	u	t		spaces	a		r	q / .			spaces		

PRINTER'S TYPE CASE

These studies of the frequency of letters were made by counting thousands upon thousands of words. They hold true for any normal message of about a thousand words. Even for messages as short as two hundred words the chances are good that the letters will appear as given. But a three-word message – SOUP COOKS SLOWLY, for example – might not follow the average frequency at all.

This leads to a very important point. No matter what substitution system is used or how expert you may be, deciphering very short messages is a difficult and often impossible task. Unless the message is about fifty words long, the chances of success are slim, unless luck favours you.

This warning is essential because the frequency table of letters is the key to use in deciding if you are dealing with a substitution or transposition cipher. Of course, your message may look like this:

?×; ?;* /-&; £;

Then there is no doubt that signs have been substituted for letters. But if letters have been used, the frequency table can be your guide. Take the coded message and make a frequency breakdown. Count the number of As, Bs, Cs, etc, right through the message. Total them up. When you have finished counting, you have the facts before you. Suppose the ten most common letters in the message you are trying to break are the following:

G	59	W	30
K	45	Q	27
Z	36	M	27
B	34	T	22
P	32	C	15

The most common letters should be E, T, A, O, N, etc, and since these do not appear among the most common letters you have found, it's quite evident that other letters have been substituted for them. Possibly G for E, K for T, and Z for A. Try these as a beginning, because you can be reasonably sure you are dealing with a substitution code.

Suppose your frequency analysis gives you these results:

E	30	N	15
T	24	O	15
A	18	R	12

You need go no further. The frequency in the text follows the normal frequency closely enough for you to be sure that the letters have been changed in *position* only. You are dealing with a transposition code.

Simple types of substitution codes are the easiest codes to break. If the message is long enough, the frequency of the letters gives you an important clue in starting. You will be helped further by other clues which expert code breakers have worked out in their study of English words and messages. For example, more than 50% of all English words begin with the letters T, A, O, S, or W. More than 50% of all English words end in the letters E, S, D, or T.

When F is the final letter of a word, it is usually preceded by O. When H is the final letter it is often preceded by G. When G is a final letter it is frequently part of the group ING. All these clues help you find the meaning of words that don't seem to have any.

The study of the words used in English and the letters that make them up goes much further. Certain letters often occur together. These the code expert calls *bigrams* or *digrams*. Everyone knows how common the combination TH is, in such words as *that, think, another, through, birth*. Combinations which occur quite often, listed roughly in order of their use, are (reading down the columns):

TH	IN	ES	OR
HE	ON	EN	TI
AN	AT	OF	HI
RE	ND	TE	AS
ER	ST	ED	TO

You may have noticed that in these twenty most common groups of two letters some are the reverse of others. This gives an additional clue. Common reversals include:

ER	and	RE
ES	and	SE
AN	and	NA
TI	and	IT
ON	and	NO

Another kind of two-letter group consists of doubled letters. The ten most frequently doubled letters in English are:

LL	FF
EE	RR
SS	NN
OO	PP
TT	CC

Groups of three letters are very common, too. Some of these include the two-letter groups just listed. Some of the three-letter groups are words. So are a few of the two-letter groups, for that matter. Here are the most common groups of three letters as they occur in normal English words:

THE	FOR	VER	ERS
ING	TIO	TER	HIS
AND	ERE	THA	RES
ION	HER	ATI	ILL
ENT	ATE	HAT	ARE

The words themselves are not important clues. They are usually disguised in the five-letter code 'words', so that true words do not begin to appear till there are enough clues to crack the cipher. At this point knowing the most common words is a help. The most common word in English is *the* and because it is so common and contains two of the three top-frequency letters, it is often left out of code messages, which usually make fairly good sense without it. Doesn't BOY STOOD ON BURNING DECK tell you the same thing as THE BOY STOOD ON THE BURNING DECK?

The most common two-letter words are:

OF	BE	HE	IF
TO	AS	BY	ME
IN	AT	OR	MY
IT	SO	ON	UP
IS	WE	DO	AN

The most common three-letter words are:

THE	NOT	HAD	OUT
AND	YOU	HER	DAY
FOR	ALL	WAS	GET
ARE	ANY	ONE	HAS
BUT	CAN	OUR	HIM

The most common four-letter words are:

THAT	YOUR	BEEN	VERY
WITH	FROM	GOOD	WHEN
HAVE	THEY	MUCH	COME
THIS	KNOW	SOME	HERE
WILL	WANT	TIME	JUST

So much for help from studying words. All the rest must come from your own thinking and your own experience. As with all code work, practice is essential. As you try breaking codes, you will learn to grasp the combination of letters that paves the way to cracking the message. The frequency table is the main tool in cracking substitution codes. It will tell you what letter probably stands for E. Remember, however, that you can't be positive that E is the most frequent letter in a short message. You may also get good clues about T, A, and O. Then by using the groups of two or three letters one gains a few more clues and each new clue makes the task easier. Perhaps an example of a specially made simple substitution code will show how to go about it.

Suppose a dark man with a turned-up collar and a turned-down hat slides up to you some dark night, pushes a paper into your hand, jumps into a black sedan and drives away. Before turning the paper over to Scotland Yard, you take a look at it. All you read is:

BDA BDEFBAAC BDEC HAC GFA GFHECI

So you take the paper home, lock your door, pull down the blinds, get out paper and pencil, and quietly go to work. First you make a frequency table and arrive at the following:

A	5 times	F	3 times
B	4 ,,	G	2 ,,
C	4 ,,	H	2 ,,
D	3 ,,	I	1 time
E	3 ,,		

Total of 27 letters

The table makes it clear that you have a substitution cipher, and a very odd one. Since A is the most frequent letter you guess it stands for E and so you begin by writing E over every A in the code:

```
E         EE          E      E
BDA BDEFBAAC BDEC HAC GFA GFHECI
```

T should be the second most common letter in the message and so it should be represented by either B or C, for each is present four times. Which is it? This takes thought and perhaps a bit of guessing. Note that three out of four Bs occur in the digram group BD at the beginning of words. The Cs are usually at the ends of words. The most common digram is TH which, if it fits the combination BD, gives us a clue to two letters at once. If we try this guess, we are rewarded in finding that the first word of our message is THE, a common enough word. This confirms our choice. B probably stands for T and D for H. Enter both on the worksheet, which now shows:

```
THE TH   TEE   TH      E      E
BDA BDEFBAAC BDEC HAC GFA GFHECI
```

C is the letter worth tackling next. Note that three words end in C and that it occurs twice in the digram EC. Looking at the digram list for two-letter groups that do *not* contain TH or E, we find the most common are AN, IN, ON, and ND. But the C is the last letter of the digram and also at the end of words, so ND can be discarded for a while and we can assume that C may be N, with a chance that E is either A, I, or O. If C *is* N, the long second word will end in TEEN. That immediately suggests a number, or rather, *the* number THIRTEEN. This, if correct, confirms that E stands for I and F stands for R. That is a big step forward and the message now reads:

```
THE THIRTEEN THIN EN    RE  R IN
BDA BDEFBAAC BDEC HAC GFA GFHECI
```

You have made real progress, faster than normal because this example is especially easy. All that are left to decipher are G, H, and I. The fifth word might be a good place to begin the last lap. It is a three-letter word that ends in RE. The table of three-letter words will help and you can also run through the alphabet for a suitable first letter. You don't have to go far because there is every chance that the word is ARE. You also have A as the opening letter of the last word. You are dealing with THE THIRTEEN THIN —EN. What does the blank stand for? Run through the alphabet. Not DEN or FEN or HEN. MEN – could very well be! Unless it is PEN or TEN. If H does stand for M, our last word becomes ARMIN—, and the answer is clear in an instant. THE THIRTEEN THIN MEN ARE ARMING. That may be a job for the police. Anyhow the code has been broken. If the dark man with the turned-up collar slips you another message in the same code, your task will be much easier next time.

If you have followed the example, you have an idea how to go about breaking a substitution code message. The very simple example didn't reveal the whole code, but having broken this much the next message would be easy and would yield a few more letters. In code breaking one is bound to make errors because one must guess and feel the way. But when you've had your first success the effort will seem worthwhile. Since success can only come from actually trying, here are three messages to break. They are all substitution codes, all simple. Each has a few clues to help.

I. FWFSZUIJOH UIBU DBNF IFSF JT PO IBOE
   Clues: Watch for digrams such as UI and FS.

The two 2-letter words will help also. Watch for ideas that will show the system used. It's a very easy one.

2. GZUD DZBG ZFDMS SZJD MNSD NE SGHR
   Clues: First and final letters of words will help. Note three peculiar combinations ZUD, ZFD, and ZJD. They should help.

3. ELMWPD ZQ WPEEPCD LCP ESP ZYWJ LTO TY MCPLVTYR NZOPD
   Clues: Note the endings PD, the reversals PC and CP, and the double letters EE. The group TY which is also a word should be a real help.

When your study of a code shows that E is the most common letter with T, A, O, and N following, you probably have a transposition code. The frequency table is no longer any help. You must now work at discovering the system on which the code is set up. This is a very slow process and may take a great deal of work. But when you have discovered the system, you have all of it. You can go right through the message at once without having to work your way letter by letter.

Transposition codes are based on the multiplication table idea (see Chapter 5). The first step in breaking this type of code is to find out what pattern may have been used. The clue to this is the number of letters in the code message. Count carefully, as an error here will spoil all your work. Suppose your message has 64 letters. That fact alone tells you it can be encoded in five ways:

$$2 \times 32 \quad 4 \times 16 \quad 8 \times 8 \quad 16 \times 4 \quad 32 \times 2$$

In this case there are five clear possibilities. Other messages may have more. But, whatever the number, there is nothing to do but try each one. Copy the message in each pattern from 2×32 right up to 32×2, and study each one in detail as you write it out. If the message is a simple transposition, you can read it down the columns as soon as you have reached the right pattern. But the transposition may be *reversed, spiral, diagonal*, and if no message appears as you go down the columns, you must try all the other routes through the message. This is slow, painfully slow, work. But it can be even harder when a code number or code word is used (see pages 65–8) and the columns are not even in normal order.

Once again a very simple example will help show how to tackle this kind of code. The message which you have to decipher merely says:

TTOWHOTEEOHANKETHAREENSR

You have no indication of word length or of the cipher used. So you immediately make a frequency table of the letters in the code and find:

E	5	N	2
T	4	R	2
O	3	S	1
H	3	W	1
A	2	K	1

Total 24 letters

The frequency of the letters in the message is so close to E, T, A, O, N, R, I, S, H, especially in such a short message, that you have good reason to believe you are

dealing with a transposition code. Your next step is
to decide on the possible patterns into which a 24-
letter message could be sent. They are 2×12, 4×6,
6×4, and 12×2.

Now the only thing left to do is to set the message
up according to these patterns and scan each one for
any words or combinations of letters that begin to
make sense. In this case we have only four patterns to
try. Remember that the pattern for decoding is the
reverse of that used in encoding. So begin by assuming
that the message was encoded on a 2×12 pattern. To
decode we set it up as 12×2, which means 12 groups
of 2 letters each. Set one beneath the other, the groups
form two columns which look like this:

```
T  T
O  W
H  O
T  E
E  O
H  A
N  K
E  T
H  A
R  E
E  N
S  R
```

Reading down the columns discloses no message
except such words as *to, woe* and *oak*. The message was
probably not encoded in a 2×12 pattern.

However, the opposite pattern, 12×2, might have
been used and to decode it we set it up as 2×12. This
gives 2 groups of 12 letters each, forming twelve short
columns:

T T O W H O T E E O H A
N K E T H A R E E N S R

Reading down the columns again gives such odd words as *oat*, *tree*, and *on*, but nothing like a message. These words were formed by accident. You can now be fairly sure that neither the 2×12 nor the 12×2 pattern was used. That leaves the 4×6 and the 6×4. Trying the 4×6 pattern, we break the message up into 6 groups of 4 letters each and write them one below the other. This gives:

T T O W
H O T E
E O H A
N K E T
H A R E
E N S R

As you look down the columns, words begin to appear at once: THEN and HE and in a jiffy you have the hidden message:

THEN HE TOOK ANOTHER SWEATER

Perhaps you wonder why such a message had to be hidden in code. So do I. At least we have deciphered a transposition message.

The two simple examples in this chapter are the best explanation of how codes are broken and why practice and skill are so essential in breaking them. Knowing how to break codes is one thing; breaking them is quite another. At least it's fun trying, and perhaps sooner or later you will develop enough skill to make cryptanalysis a real hobby.

HELPS FOR CODE BREAKERS

Here are the letters of the alphabet arranged in order of the frequency of their occurrence in English words:

ETAONRISHDLFCMUGYPWBVKXJQZ

More than 50% of all English words *begin* with the letters T, A, O, S, or W. More than 50% of all English words *end* with the letters E, S, D, T. Watch for *bigrams* and *digrams*. In order of frequency the most common are:

TH HE AN RE ER IN ON AT ND ST ES EN
OF TE ED OR TI HI AS TO

Note the most common reversed letters:

ER and RE
ES and SE
AN and NA
TI and IT
ON and NO

Doubled letters in order of their occurrence:

LL EE SS OO TT FF RR NN PP CC

The most common two-letter words in English are:

OF	TO	IN	IS	IT
BE	AS	AT	SO	WE
HE	BY	OR	ON	DO
IF	ME	MY	UP	AN

The most common three-letter words:

THE	AND	FOR	ARE	BUT
NOT	YOU	ALL	ANY	CAN
HAD	HER	WAS	ONE	OUR
OUT	DAY	GET	HAS	HIM

The most common four-letter words:

THAT	WITH	HAVE	THIS	WILL
YOUR	FROM	THEY	KNOW	WANT
BEEN	GOOD	MUCH	SOME	TIME
VERY	WHEN	COME	HERE	JUST

SEVEN

Special Codes and Secret Languages

Peter Livingston, who was only ten at the time, planned the whole thing with me. It took about six weeks of practice and then we were ready. Peter, facing all the pupils, sat alone on the platform. At the back of the auditorium I asked a boy to pick a coin from a handful and look at the date. 'Peter', I called out, 'concentrate on the date of this coin. Think carefully. What is it?'

Peter thought a moment and answered, '1941'. He was right. We tried another coin and then another. Two 'judges' blindfolded Peter, but every time I asked him to think and urged him along, he came through with the answer.

Then I asked a girl to write her age and birthday on a slip of paper. I looked at it, folded and sealed it in an envelope, and gave it to one of the judges. 'Now, Peter,' I called. 'Think of this girl's age. Don't guess. Now think of the month she was born. Go slowly. Think hard. And now concentrate on the date. Take your time.'

'She is twelve years old and was born on May 9th,' Peter said.

The judge opened the envelope and, sure enough, the note read: 'I was born on May 9th and I'm twelve years old.'

Peter, blindfolded, could name colours when people pointed to them on a chart. He could tell the colour of a boy's sweater and a girl's dress and the addresses where they lived. Everyone was mystified, and even those who thought they knew the secret could not put their finger on Peter's amazing ability. You have probably guessed from the title of this chapter that a code was used. So it was. Peter and I worked out a special code which suited our purpose very well. That, plus the way we went about the demonstration, had most of the audience fooled.

Many kinds of special codes exist. Most are simple and provide secrecy for some special use, not for sending the usual kinds of messages. Have you noticed the price-tags when shopping? You may have seen something like ARC or DBE instead of a price. The shopkeeper's code is one of these special types. For a key, select a ten-letter word in which no letter is repeated. Then each letter will stand for a number from one to nine, and the last will stand for zero. Words like *artichokes* or *dumbwaiter* are good ones to use in such a code.

```
1 2 3 4 5 6 7 8 9 0
D U M B W A I T E R
```

With this code a ball costing 1/6d would be marked D/A and a bat for 10/3d would be encoded DR/M. You may want to take the trouble to make note of several coded prices and then ask the price of the items you have noted down. With these facts you may have enough information to 'break' the shopkeeper's code. However, in a store the *cost* price only may be marked on the tag in code. When a price is given to a customer, enough money is added to clear expenses and make a profit. Thus an article marked U/T (2/8d) might sell for five shillings, in order for the merchant to meet his costs and make a profit.

Jumping from Peter's demonstration to the store's code is only to show that codes involving numbers have many uses. Many 'mind-reading' codes are the kind that involve numbers. Each digit is represented by a word instead of by a letter as in the shopkeeper's code. The words used must be chosen with care. They must be common enough to fit into what might normally be said at the time without arousing suspicion. Here is a code like the one we used in our demonstration.

1 HURRY	6 NOW
2 THINK	7 UNDERSTAND
3 MORE	8 AGAIN
4 QUICK	9 TRY
5 TIME	0 GUESS

These words, carefully woven into the conversation, gave Peter the clues he needed. When I said, 'Peter, what coin am I holding in my hand? Think hard. Do you know now?' Peter knew it was half a crown. The words, *think* and *now*, were the clues that stood for 2/6d. If I had a ten-shilling note I might have said, 'Hurry up, but don't guess.' *Hurry* and *guess* are 10. When Peter wasn't sure of the clues, he'd indicate that by saying: 'There's too much noise. I can't concentrate.' Or he would ask me to concentrate harder. Then I'd repeat the clues in some different sentence.

For the girl who was twelve years old on May 9th, the clues consisted of words to indicate she was twelve, such as '*Hurry* up and *think* of her age.' Then another clue gave the month. May is the fifth month and the clue might be, 'This *time* concentrate on the month she was born. *Try* to get the date, too.' The words *time* and *try* meant fifth month, ninth day.

We worked other codes on the same words. If the question had anything to do with colour, *hurry* (1) stood for yellow; *think* (2) for orange; *more* (3) for blue; *quick* (4) for green; *time* (5) for red, etc. '*Hurry* up and tell me the colour of this boy's tie. See how *quick* you can be.' And Peter, still blindfolded, would take the clue from *hurry* and *quick* and reply, 'He's wearing a yellow and green tie.'

With this much of an idea as to how such codes are made and used, go ahead and try your own. Once again, practice is important. Unless everything said sounds natural, the code is weak. Never say the code word louder or with more emphasis than any other words. Develop a 'patter', so that people are used to hearing you talk as you go. This will give you more opportunity to hide the code words. Then, when you have mastered this code and people challenge you to do your demonstration without talking, you can look up and try the code that signals the numbers from one to nine by different positions of the head.

One could list many other kinds of special codes, but such a list might easily lead a person astray, since there is no clear line between codes, ciphers and signs, symbols, abbreviations, and other special marks. Codes and code signals are used at sea, on railways, in radio, and in a number of other important activities. The main purpose of these signs and symbols is not secrecy, but a quick, simple way of conveying information. If you saw two flags flying from a high Florida tower, both red squares with black squares in the centre, you might think them odd. But a native would start for home immediately to nail everything down. He'd know a hurricane signal on sight.

Insignia on planes and the funnel marks on ships tell those who know to what country the plane belongs and who owns the ship. These signs and symbols are rarely intended to be secret. Cattle brands are another type of sign which only the initiated can understand. The astronomer, mathematician, and chemist all use symbols which might seem mysterious or secret to you, unless you studied the subject. Yet these symbols express ideas more clearly than words. Symbols are used in showing electric and radio circuits. Engineers put marks on maps which might seem designs to you, but which tell the engineer a good deal about the land, rivers, houses, and other features. Not all these signs and symbols are put down in writing. If you have ever watched a football game, you know how the referee and other officials use hand signals. The umpire at a tennis game and the policeman on the corner use hand signals, too. So did the Red Indians with their sign language. Deaf and dumb people can talk rapidly by the same method.

To go into all the other kinds of signs and symbols to which codes are related would be a long task; but secret languages are another matter. Secret languages are rare things, and most interesting. Languages are the way we pass on ideas from one person to another. When more people understand the language, it becomes less and less secret. But if two professors held a conversation in Sanskrit, they would, to all purposes, have a secret language, because Sanskrit is not spoken by any living people and only a few students know it. Yet Sanskrit was used at one time, and so it was never meant to be a true secret language.

A secret language is one that is designed for secrecy

and is used in addition to the language people ordinarily speak. Such secondary languages are widely used. At one period, the French language was the accepted tongue in all the courts of Europe. Only the peasants and tradesmen spoke Russian or German or Spanish. The nobles used French. Sometime earlier, Latin had held the same position that French later occupied. But these were snobbish languages, not really secret ones.

ISTENLAY YMAY HILDRENCAY ANDWAY
OUYAY HALLSAY EARHAY
OFWAY HETAY IDNIGHTMAY IDERAY OFWAY
AULPAY EVERERAY.

These two lines of a poem which you all know are in a secret language which you have certainly heard, even if you don't know it on sight: Pig Latin. Even the name is something secret, since the language has even less to do with Latin than with pigs. Though Pig Latin is a real secret language, it is actually known by millions of people who use it to some extent. But only a few really get the practice to make themselves Pig-Latin experts. Simple though Pig Latin is, outsiders find it hard even to follow the words when it is spoken rapidly. Like code breaking, Pig Latin or any other secret language is easy to explain or understand, but it takes a good deal of practice to get the skill to use it well. Every year thousands of people learn Pig Latin. If you don't know it, Pig Latin can be mastered quite quickly.

Pig Latin is based on good, ordinary English, the kind we use every day. To change English into Pig Latin, only two methods are used. Both are so easy that, with practice, of course, you can translate as you go. To all words beginning with a vowel (A, E, I, O,

U) merely add the syllable WAY. Thus ARE becomes AREWAY, EAT becomes EATWAY, OVER becomes OVERWAY. Spoken singly these words are easy to recognize, but mixed with other words they are not. The second method deals with words that begin with consonants, all letters that are not vowels. To change such words into Pig Latin, the first letter is moved to the end of the word and then the syllable AY is added. MAN shifts the M and adds AY to the end, becoming ANMAY. Move the C of CAT to the end, add AY, and it becomes ATCAY in Pig Latin. HETAY ATCAY ISWAY ICKSAY — THE CAT IS SICK. Once you get the hang of it, the change is simple: BOOK to OOKBAY; PEN to ENPAY; ICE CREAM to ICEWAY REAMCAY.

This is about all there is to Pig Latin. However, exceptions occur every now and then when a word becomes very awkward to handle in the usual way. Here it is hard to lay down rules, because people work these problems out for themselves. Possibly the best example of an exception which everyone knows is the word AMSCRAY which is Pig Latin for SCRAM. Normally, SCRAM should become CRAMSAY, but it seemed better to shift the first three letters instead of only the first one; hence AMSCRAY. A word like SOMEONE becomes a tongue twister in Pig Latin: OMEONESAY. In this case, shifting the first syllable is easier and you get ONESOMAY. Try to avoid the exceptions if you can. Keep your Pig Latin simple and it will be fun without getting you snarled.

Pig Latin is a spoken language. You'll find no books written in Pig Latin, nor will you want to write Pig Latin notes. But, since practice is important, here is some Pig Latin to translate. An even better kind of practice is to find someone who also wants to learn

Pig Latin and start talking together, with short, simple sentences at first and then more and faster as you gain skill. Translate the following into Pig Latin:

1. PIG LATIN IS THE EASIEST AND MOST WIDELY USED SECRET LANGUAGE.
2. A MAN WHO HAS STUDIED SECRET LANGUAGES SAYS THAT GIRLS LEARN AND USE PIG LATIN MUCH EASIER AND MORE OFTEN THAN BOYS.
3. IN THE MIDDLE AGES, LATIN WAS THE LANGUAGE OF SCHOLARS AND LEARNED PEOPLE. IT WAS THE LANGUAGE USED IN TEACHING AND IN WHICH MOST BOOKS WERE WRITTEN.

Read these Pig Latin sentences:

4. HETAY AVERAGEWAY ENGTHLAY OFWAY ORDSWAY INWAY HETAY ENGLISHWAY ANGUAGELAY ISWAY ABOUTWAY OURFAY ANDWAY AWAY ALFHAY ETTERSLAY.
5. INWAY ALLWAY HETAY OMMONCAY ANGUAGESLAY OFWAY ESTERNWAY EUROPEWAY ANDWAY AMERICAWAY EWAY ISWAY HETAY ETTERLAY HATTAY ISWAY USEDWAY HETAY OSTMAY OFTENWAY.
6. ORDSWAY IKELAY ADDEDWAY, ASSESPAY, ERRORWAY, ORWAY EEMEDSAY AREWAY OTNAY OODGAY OTAY USEWAY INWAY ODESCAY ECAUSEBAY HETAY EPEATEDRAY ETTERSLAY AYMAY IVEGAY HETAY LUECAY ONWAY HICHWAY HETAY ODECAY ANCAY EBAY ROKENBAY

No other secret language is as well known as Pig

Latin. In this country, about a half-dozen are known and used. Some work on about the same idea as Pig Latin. Others are more complicated. Turkey Irish uses the Pig-Latin idea and is even simpler than Pig Latin. Words are made by putting AB before every vowel. In Turkey Irish RUN becomes RABUN and GIRL is GABIRL. BRING THE SWEETS TO THE SECRET CAVE is translated into BRABING THABE SWABEETS TABO THABE SABECRABET CABAVABE. Words with a number of vowels may cause trouble, but take them as they sound rather than as they are spelled.

Opish is another simple language in which an extra syllable is added to English words. It, too, is simpler than Pig Latin, since only one method of changing words is used. In Opish you add the syllable OP after each consonant. The word GIRL in Opish is GOPIROPLOP and CAT is COPATOP. This turns a word like UM-BRELLA into UMOPBOPROPELLOPA. Note that when consonants are repeated like the LL in UM-BRELLA, OP is added after the pair, so it becomes LLOP instead of LOPLOP. That is all there is to Opish. If you prefer it to Turkey Irish or Pig Latin, you are welcome to it. Since all three of these secret languages are based on the same idea, a quick comparison will give you the essential facts about them all.

Language and Principle	*Examples*
PIG LATIN	
Add WAY to words beginning with a vowel. For words beginning with a consonant, move the consonant to the end and add AY	CAT ATCAY EVENT EVENTWAY SALE ALESAY

TURKEY IRISH

Add AB before every
vowel

CAT CABAT

EVENT ABEVABENT

SALE SABALABE

OPISH

Add OP after every con-
sonant

CAT COPATOP

EVENT EVOPENOPTOP

SALE SOPALOPE

With all three secret languages lined up you can see the advantages and disadvantages of each. For my own use, I'll take Pig Latin, but perhaps that is only because I knew it first and had something of a start. Another secret language is common enough to be worthy of mention.

Double Dutch is a much more complicated secret language than those just mentioned because more changes are introduced. Instead of repeating a single syllable, Double Dutch substitutes a whole new set of consonants. Vowels remain the same and are pronounced as usual, but the consonants are replaced by a series of syllables which include the consonants and which confuse outsiders:

B	BUB	K	KUK	S	SUS
C	CASH	L	LUL	T	TUT
D	DUD	M	MUM	V	VUX
F	FUF	N	NUN	W	WASH
G	GUG	P	PUP	X	XUX
H	HUTCH	Q	QUACK	Y	YUB
J	JUG	R	RUG	Z	ZUB

In this Double Dutch, CAT becomes CASHATUT; EVENT is EVUVENUNTUT and SALE is SUSALUL. HOW ARE YOU? ends up as HUTCHOWASH

ARUGE YUBOU? You can be sure that Double Dutch is more difficult to master than the languages just mentioned, but some people prefer it.

So much for secret languages, though this is far from the end. With these examples in mind you can invent languages of your own. Many secret languages are invented every day and many are used by young people in other countries. My wife remembers as a child in Russia she and her friends used a language something like Opish and Turkey Irish.

In the Russian version a consonant (such as P) was added after every *sounded* vowel (or vowel group) and then the vowel was repeated. CAT became CAPAT, but BIG changed to BIPIG, and COT to COPOT. When two vowels occur together as in BOAT, they are repeated as a group: BOAPOAT. E at the end of a word when it has no sound (as in LIKE, RATTLE, or GRAPE) does not change. The sentence NO GIRLS CAN COME TO THE MEETING becomes NOPO GIPIRLS CAPAN COPOME TOPO THEPE MEEPEE-TIPING. The consonants can be changed from day to day: P on Monday, K on Tuesday, R on Wednesday, and so on. With these changes the word LAMP would change from LAPAMP to LAKAMP, to LARAMP.

Seriously, secret languages are fun, but they should not be considered as anything more than fun. The only reason that Pig Latin or Double Dutch works at all is because each is built entirely on the English language, with just a few trimmings to hide the familiar sounds of familiar words. Inventing a new language is a tremendous task, as you will appreciate if you ever study language enough to see in what detail a language is built. But for fun and for saying secret things that younger brothers and sisters can't understand, the secret languages are just the thing.

EIGHT

Secret Writing

Given the time and enough messages, an expert can break almost any code. That makes it quite important to see that code messages do not go astray. Written code messages have been disguised with innocent-looking letters, in pictures, and in designs. Secret writing with invisible inks is often used to help put the message into the hands of the person who should receive it and no one else. Used with codes, secret writing adds another step in security, for while an ordinary code may arouse suspicion, an invisible one certainly will not. And, since secret writing works so well, codes may be omitted and the message can still be a secret one.

Like codes, secret writing may often be very difficult, requiring rare or dangerous chemicals or the use of ultra-violet light. It can be a study for experts. But there are also ways of doing secret writing with simple materials that are safe and cheap. This chapter and the next contain this information. It would be a simple matter to list the formulae for making invisible inks and other materials for secret writing. But it is just as important to understand how and why these chemicals work. Such knowledge will help prevent mistakes and may also aid you in experimenting to invent your own kinds of invisible inks.

The how and why of secret writing takes us back to the chemical elements of which the earth is made.

There are ninety-two of these elements, plus others which scientists have learned to make by the use of atomic power. We will not need any of these new man-made elements for secret writing. In fact, only a dozen or so of the old-fashioned natural kind are needed. These include elements such as iron, copper, lead, sodium, sulphur, iodine, and carbon which are found in the earth and in the seas. The ones you will use may come from the kitchen shelf, the medicine cabinet, and perhaps from the grocery or chemist shop.

Very few of the ninety-two elements are found or used in their pure form. We use copper in making electric wires. Sometimes we use pure carbon, pure sulphur, or pure lead. But most elements we find and use are joined with one, two, or three other elements, forming what the chemist calls a compound. There are many, many more compounds than elements, and most secret writing is done with chemical compounds. Some of these compounds are so common that you know and can name a dozen or so yourself. Table salt is a chemical compound, so are sugar, baking soda, lye, water, and ammonia.

Things are either elements or compounds or mixtures of these two. Often these mixtures are so complicated they are difficult to understand, and many of them are so complex that the chemist cannot duplicate them in the laboratory. Air, ink, milk, bread, and wood are mixtures of compounds. All living things are mixtures, so complicated that they must be put in a group by themselves. Yet elements and compounds are the building blocks of which they are made. In some secret writing these mixtures of compounds, usually from living things, are used as 'inks'.

Chemists know and work with thousands upon

thousands of chemical compounds, no two of which are exactly the same. Every day new and different compounds are made. Some are as common as sand, some as valuable as rubies, as deadly as cyanide, and as tasty as sugar. Some are coloured, some are colourless. Some are hard, some are soft. Put a spoonful of sugar, a compound, into a glass of water. Stir and it seems to disappear or dissolve in the water. There is no way you can tell by looking at the glass of water that there is sugar in it. You can tell immediately by tasting, but not by looking. Elements and compounds which dissolve in water are *soluble*. In secret writing, soluble compounds are usually the chemicals used. These are the kind which, dissolved in water, flow easiest from a pen. Some soluble compounds are coloured, like those in ordinary ink. These are of no use in secret writing. The compounds for secret writing must be *soluble* and *colourless*. If one writes carefully with such a compound, there will be no trace of it on the paper when the ink dries.

But secret writing is of no value unless there is some way to make it visible again. Write a long letter with a pen dipped in water, and once the water has dried your message will remain secret for ever, even to yourself. Nothing can be done to make it visible again. But if you wrote with a colourless chemical solution of *lead nitrate*, then your friend, who knows the secret, could make the invisible writing appear as yellow or black. If he treated the lead chemical writing with a compound that contained iodine, the writing would appear yellow. Treat it with a compound containing sulphur, and the invisible writing will appear black.

If you take some pictures with a camera and then take the roll of film into a dark-room, you can examine it in a dull red light. When you do, you will see nothing on the film to show that a picture has been taken. Exposed and unexposed film look exactly the same. But if you pass the exposed film through a solution of chemicals called *developer*, the picture soon appears. A developer is needed for secret writing also. It may not be the same developer used in photography, but it does the same job – that of making the invisible visible.

With secret writing you must have the right kind of developer. The developer for one kind of writing may not work at all with another, and may, in fact, spoil the secret writing so that it can never be developed. The person who is to receive the secret message must know which developer to use. If the chemical used in the writing is changed, he must be told so that he can change to the correct developer.

The developer is usually another chemical compound, dissolved in water. When the colourless compound with which the message is written is moistened by the developing solution, the two chemicals react. In the change that takes place a *coloured*, *insoluble* compound is usually formed and, of course, the writing becomes visible. Look at a message written with a colourless lead 'ink', a dilute solution of lead nitrate. The paper seems absolutely blank. To make the message visible, the sheet of paper is placed face down in a shallow dish of water containing *sodium iodide* or a few drops of ordinary *tincture of iodine*. In the chemical reaction that takes place immediately, the lead nitrate unites with the iodine, forming a yellow insoluble compound, lead iodide, which makes the writing visible.

Here are some good invisible inks and the liquid developers needed to make them visible:

INK	DEVELOPER
Copper sulphate (blue vitriol), $\frac{1}{8}$ teaspoon to a glass of water	Sodium iodide, 2 teaspoons to a glass of water

Copper sulphate is invisible only when used in very dilute solution. Hence a stronger developer is needed. The message appears brown and tests give clear results with very little blurring.

INK	DEVELOPER
Copper sulphate (blue vitriol), 1 teaspoon to a glass of water	Sodium carbonate (washing soda), 2 teaspoons to a glass of water

The ink develops into a light blue colour. These two chemicals are the safest, cheapest, and easiest to get for ordinary use in secret writing.

INK	DEVELOPER
Copper sulphate (blue vitriol), 1 teaspoon to a glass of water	Ammonium hydroxide (household ammonia), 2 teaspoons to a glass of water

Ink develops to a dark blue colour but may blur because it becomes soluble.

INK	DEVELOPER
Lead nitrate (sugar of lead), $\frac{1}{2}$ teaspoon to a glass of water	Sodium iodide, 1 teaspoon to a glass of water

Develops bright yellow, does not blur easily.

INK	DEVELOPER
Lead nitrate (sugar of lead), $\frac{1}{2}$ teaspoon to a glass of water	Sodium sulphide, $\frac{1}{2}$ teaspoon to a glass of water

Develops into a shiny black. This is a very sensitive ink and developer.

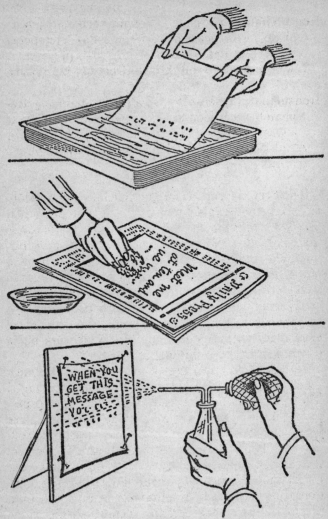

LIQUID DEVELOPERS
CAN BE DIPPED, DAUBED, OR SPRAYED

INK	DEVELOPER
Iron sulphate (ferrous sulphate), 1 teaspoon to a glass of water	Sodium carbonate (washing soda), 2 teaspoons to a glass of water

Ink develops as a dull brown. Does not blur easily.

INK	DEVELOPER
Iron sulphate (ferrous sulphate), 1 teaspoon to a glass of water	Sodium sulphide, $\frac{1}{2}$ teaspoon to a glass of water

A satisfactory combination which develops as brown writing.

These seven formulae for invisible inks and developers need some explanation as the first step in their use. These formulae have been put down first because the combination of two chemicals to form a visible, insoluble chemical (the chemist would call it a *precipitate*) is the easiest to understand. Other kinds of secret writing are sometimes easier to use, but are not easier to understand. The reaction between the two compounds is simple enough, and any student of elementary chemistry can go ahead and work out a dozen or more possibilities.

In actual practice, use of an invisible ink which requires a liquid developer has some disadvantages. The message cannot be read till the developer is prepared, and that usually means taking it to some place where one can work alone. Also liquids are apt to spill and may soil clothing unless you are careful. None of the chemicals mentioned can be considered dangerous unless one is so rash as to drink the developing solutions, but they can be a nuisance when dripped on a suit or spilled on the best rug. Besides all this, some skill is required in preparing and using the developer.

But a few words on the ink are in order before we

get too involved in the developer. You need much less ink than developer, so it may be enough to make up one quarter or one half of the amount listed, using the chemicals in the correct strength. Though some of the ink chemicals are coloured, they are practically invisible when used in dilute solution. There is little chance of seeing them after the ink has dried. This is especially true if the secret message is hidden between the lines of some other 'innocent' message. In such a case be sure that the ink used in the innocent message won't smudge the entire paper when it is put in the developer. Writing between the lines of a typewritten message is best. Or use a waterproof ink.

In writing a secret message, use an old fountain pen or some other pen with a smooth point. A scratchy pen will leave marks behind and the scratches may give your message away. A final precaution: if possible avoid ordinary steel pens. The iron in them may react with the chemical ink and spoil your results.

A message written carefully with invisible ink cannot be detected even when held up to the light or otherwise examined. It takes the developer to bring the message out. In making the developer, be sure that the chemical is completely dissolved. All these chemicals dissolve faster in warm water than cold. Within the limits of cost, use as concentrated a developer as possible. This will save time, give better results, and help to keep the message from becoming blurred. You will need a container for the developer, of course. This may be an old dinner plate, an enamelled pan, or a photographer's tray. Glass or enamel are best to use. A metal dish may react with the chemical in the developer.

It's a good idea to use as little developer as possible. There is no need to make a bucketful when a glassful will do just as well. The amounts given in the formula are level teaspoons to a drinking glass (8 ounces) of water. The solution may be made more dilute by using less of the chemical. Experiment for yourself. In general, it is wise to keep the ink solution as dilute as possible, so there will be less chance of any marks showing on the paper. The developer can then be made more concentrated to bring the writing out. On this point, try it for yourself. If the ink is made too dilute, the chances of making the message visible will be spoilt. You can use more dilute inks on some kinds of paper than on others, but these details can only be worked out by trial and error.

The tricks of good developing will come as you practise. If possible, the developing pan should be larger than the sheet of paper with the message, though the developer need only cover the bottom of the pan for a $\frac{1}{4}$-inch or so. Lay the message face down in the developer. Do not stir or move the paper. The reaction should take place immediately, and the paper can be lifted out and laid down flat on a sheet of newspaper or a large blotter. Do not hold the sheet up, as developer will run down it, smudge the message, and drip on the table. If you want to keep the message, you can blot off the excess developer carefully or else just let the paper dry slowly. When finished, pour the developer back into a bottle. Keep it corked. Then wash out your pan to remove the last traces of developer.

Another method which is just about as good is to lay the message face up on a sheet of newspaper. Moisten a bit of gauze or absorbent cotton with the developer and dab (do *not* rub) the chemical over the message. Enough solution can be applied quickly to reveal the message. This method eliminates pans

and dripping, but it does not work as well with very
dilute inks, and it is easy to blur and smudge messages
when applying the developer.

Still another method is to lay the message on newspaper and spray the developer on with an old
atomizer. If the atomizer works well and the developer
covers the message as a fine mist, the results are
admirable in most cases and the hidden message comes
out clearly. But if you have an old atomizer that drips
and spurts, the message may be spotted and blurred
before you are finished.

The reaction of the ink and developer usually
produces a coloured insoluble chemical wherever the
message is written. The fact that the chemical is
insoluble makes reading the message possible. However, there is one set of chemicals that can be used
even though the result of the reaction is a soluble
chemical. This means that more care is necessary in
developing, but the results are often worth it. For ink,
use a very concentrated solution of *phenolphthalein*
which you can buy at the chemists. A half-ounce of
this white powder is all you will need. Phenolphthalein
dissolves in water, but it will dissolve better in
methylated spirit. Keep the solution corked when not
in use. Write with phenolphthalein ink as with any
other invisible ink. Phenolphthalein can be developed
with ammonia or washing soda. Use a concentrated
solution and either dab or spray it on the message
which will be revealed in a deep blood-red. This is so
striking that it's worth trying, even though the message
will blur more than with other inks. With this same
chemical you can try other stunts like changing 'water'
(a dilute solution of phenolphthalein) into 'wine' by
pouring the solution into a glass which contains a drip
or two of ammonia.

As with codes, practice in secret writing is essential. Get your materials and go ahead. Washing soda and ammonia can be bought in any grocery, if they are not already around the house. The other chemicals may be obtained from chemists or chemical supply houses. An ounce or so of each will last you a very long time.

NINE

More and More Invisible Inks

Scientists have discovered that the simplest things are often the most difficult to understand and explain. This is true of some of the invisible inks listed in this chapter. Those developed by the use of liquid developer produce a clear-cut chemical reaction with which you are now familiar. Other kinds of chemicals may be used to produce the same type of reaction. The developer might be a powder rubbed on the message or, better still, a gas.

The use of a gas as a developer (not gas from the kitchen stove) is worth trying, if you are interested enough in chemistry to make the gases needed. A developing gas useful with a half-dozen inks is *hydrogen sulphide* – a gas with the distinct odour of rotten eggs. Hydrogen sulphide gas will develop most of the inks already listed in Chapter 8 and others, too. You can use it with copper sulphate, cobalt chloride, iron sulphate, or lead nitrate. All of these inks react with the gas and develop the message in a grey or black colour.

This gas can be made by pouring vinegar (pure white vinegar is best) on a chemical known as sodium sulphide. Since only a bit of the gas is needed, one does not require any chemical apparatus. A quart jar (or larger) with a wide mouth will do. Put a full teaspoon of the powdered sodium sulphide on the bottom, add three tablespoons of vinegar, cover the jar, and let it stand. To develop the message it is a good idea to hold the paper in the steam from a boiling kettle for a minute to moisten it slightly. Then put the paper inside the jar or over the open top, till the gas produces its effect.

Another interesting gas to use is the very poisonous gas *chlorine*. The amount you will use to develop secret writing is so small that no real danger can come from its use. A teaspoon of *calcium hypochlorite*, also known as *bleaching powder* or *chloride of lime*, placed on the bottom of a quart jar will yield a small amount of chlorine gas when vinegar is added. The jar should be kept covered. Chlorine is only useful in developing

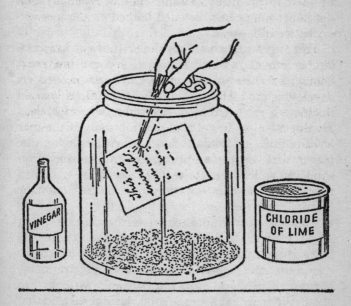

GAS DEVELOPER USED IN JAR

invisible writing made with *sodium iodide* ink. But this is an excellent ink to use, and it can be used, in a very dilute solution. The chlorine gas frees the iodine from the sodium iodide and produces a brownish colour, or bluish, if the paper contains starch.

Though the amount of chlorine formed is very small, it is a sensitive developer and this combination of sodium iodide ink and chlorine developer is a good one. Ammonia gas can also be used as a gas developer on the same inks which respond to a solution of ammonia. To use ammonia as a gas, put about a teaspoon of household ammonia into a quart jar. The liquid forms the gas readily, and you need hardly be told to keep the jar covered. Copper sulphate and iron sulphate inks respond to ammonia gas, especially after the paper has been moistened with steam.

Gas developers work, and there is little chance of blurring messages when they are used. By experimenting, if you know the principles of chemistry, some new and startling combinations with gas developers can be worked out. But, frankly, gases seldom do things which could not be done with a liquid developer.

Of all the apples in the secret-writing barrel, the biggest and best remains. One group of invisible inks needs no other chemical, either liquid or gas, as a developer. Just heating the invisible ink message makes the writing appear. The 'heat sensitive' inks are the easiest to find and use. They are safest, too, for that matter. If all this is so, 'Why,' you may ask, 'have they been kept till last?' The only reason for this is that the group includes a variety of chemical compounds and mixtures and very little is known about them as inks, outside of the simple fact that they do work and work very well.

Best known of these simple inks which become visible when heated is milk, ordinary cow's milk. Goat's milk, buttermilk, or evaporated milk may work just as well. Writing in milk is quite invisible, and when the paper with the message is heated the writing appears as a warm brown colour. The process is so simple that it's almost amazing to see the message written in milk gradually appear as the paper is warmed.

Milk is not a chemical compound but a mixture of many organic chemicals. In many ways it is like a number of other substances all obtained from living things that may be used in secret writing. The list may easily be extended, but those inks which have been tested and found satisfactory include the following:

MILK. Use directly. Avoid cream, as fat stains may result

SUGAR. Use a dilute solution. One teaspoon to a glass of water is sufficient.

LEMON JUICE, ORANGE JUICE, GRAPEFRUIT JUICE. The juices of these three citrus fruits all work well. It seems to me that orange juice gives better results than lemon. But try them for yourself.

ONION JUICE. Oddly enough, this gives excellent results and was not as bad to use as you might think. Try it.

APPLE JUICE. This worked, too, though not as well as citrus juices.

HONEY. A teaspoon of honey in a glass of water gives results very similar to sugar, and perhaps a bit better.

COCA-COLA. Believe it or not, this and other similar drinks can be used as invisible inks. They all contain sugar and work very much like sugar solutions. If colour shows in writing, dilute with water.

VINEGAR. Use directly. Makes an excellent ink.

How these inks work is an open question, but the answer probably lies in their chemical composition. All are organic compounds, compounds that contain the element carbon. Carbon as an element is black in colour, but in compounds no indication of the colour of the element exists. When a sheet of paper containing a secret message written in milk, lemon juice, or sugar water is heated, the compound is broken down by the heat, liberating the element carbon which gives the writing its characteristic brown or blackish colour. It's the same reaction as burning a pie or pancake.

There is a complication to the story, however, because the paper itself is a mixture of organic compounds which are affected the same way by heat. Heat a paper enough (taking care it doesn't burst into flame) and it will char to a brown or even black. Milk and lemon juice are good invisible inks because they are affected by heat quicker than paper, and hence the ink compounds break down to form carbon before the paper does. This makes it a good idea to write on fairly heavy paper or cards when using this type of invisible ink.

Developing an ink with heat raises another problem that cannot be overlooked. Just a moment's carelessness and you have a bonfire instead of a secret message. Heating requires care. If possible, use an electric hotplate, an electric iron, or even a large electric light bulb (150–200 watts). Next best is to use the gas stove, holding the message with a clipping kind of clothespeg, so as not to burn your fingers. A large source of

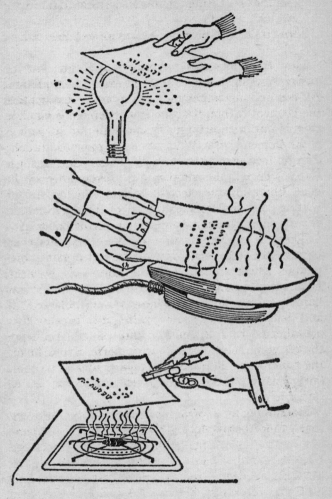

DEVELOPING SECRET WRITING WITH HEAT

heat is best. A candle or a small lamp is likely to give the poorest results unless extra care is used. In heating a message, keep the paper moving all the time, moving it nearer to the heat source as needed. If you work with an open flame, there is always a chance (though a small one) that your paper will catch on fire. If it does, just let it burn on the stove or let it drop to the floor and step on it. If your message does burn, you have lost it. So for the sake of your message, as well as for safety's sake, be careful.

Another group of chemicals makes good heat-sensitive inks. These are not organic chemicals and their action is quite different. These do not decompose easily and do not yield carbon when they do. So it is hard to say just why they work so well as invisible inks. It is quite possible that they absorb heat faster than the surface of the paper and so the paper chars more under the chemical ink of the message than elsewhere. You may find it worthwhile experimenting with these inorganic, heat-sensitive inks. The chemicals themselves are no mystery. Here are some:

SALT. A solution of 1 teaspoon to a glass of water does well. If the concentration is too great, the tiny salt crystals may be seen in the writing.

WASHING SODA. Works as well as or better than salt and seems good in even more dilute solutions.

BICARBONATE OF SODA. Also quite satisfactory.

EPSOM SALT. One teaspoon to a glass of water gives good results with strong heating.

COPPER SULPHATE. This chemical can be developed by heat as well as by the liquid developers. Use $\frac{1}{8}$ teaspoon to a glass of water.

AMMONIUM CHLORIDE. This cheap and safe chemical, obtained at any chemists, works very

well. It develops clearly and evenly on fairly
strong heating. Use ⅛ teaspoon to a glass of water,
or slightly more, if necessary.

IRON SULPHATE. The same ferrous sulphate used
with a liquid developer will also work with heat.
It doesn't seem as good as ammonium chloride,
but is worth trying.

One other group of inorganic chemicals is useful.
These are chemicals which contain an excess of oxygen. Cheapest and easiest to use is *sodium nitrate*. Use
a dilute solution, about ⅛ teaspoon to a glass of water.
On heating this ink, the chemical breaks down, freeing
some of the oxygen. Oxygen, of course, aids burning
and so the heated paper chars wherever there is any
writing. The results are clear and very distinct. As a
stunt, write with a concentrated solution of sodium
nitrate (2 teaspoons to a half-glass of water); use a
brush or absorbent cotton wound on a stick. Write on
a large sheet of wrapping paper and be sure each letter
connects to the next, as in script writing. When the
word (try a single word first) is dry, touch the beginning of the first letter with a red-hot wire or very
lightly with a match. The nitrate will break down and
the paper will start to smoulder. The burning will
continue along the path you have written and this
'magic' flame will spell out the word you wrote. People
who don't know chemistry will be mystified by the
stunt. You may have to experiment a bit to get the
right concentration of sodium nitrate, but the exciting
results will make your efforts worthwhile.

A final group of chemicals, and a small one, is
particularly interesting because after the message has
been developed by heat it disappears again as soon as
the heat is removed, or shortly thereafter. Every time

you heat the message it reappears. Every time it cools it disappears again. The chemical that shows this odd reaction best is *cobalt chloride*, which is also used as an ink with liquid developers. This chemical contains water. The solution ($\frac{1}{2}$ teaspoon to a glass of water) is a pale pink, and writing with it is practically invisible. When heated, the cobalt chloride gives up its water and, in doing so, changes from pink to blue, a blue that is deep enough to be clearly visible. The message can be read easily. But if it is put aside, the paper cools and the cobalt chloride gradually absorbs water from the air and loses its colour. In a few hours the message is invisible again.

Neither copper sulphate nor ammonium chloride gives this same effect, but a mixture of the two chemicals does. Use one teaspoon of each to a glass of water. The writing, which is quite invisible, becomes yellowish brown on heating and fades again on cooling. The results are not quite as good, however, as those produced by the cobalt chloride.

Another kind of charring is produced by chemicals with such an attraction for water that they will extract it from chemical compounds, such as paper, which are made of cellulose – carbon, hydrogen, and oxygen. When some of the hydrogen and oxygen of cellulose are removed as water, the black carbon remains. Sulphuric acid is such a compound. A drop on a piece of paper blackens the spot at once. But concentrated sulphuric acid will do the same to your skin. It is far too dangerous to use in secret writing.

Fortunately another chemical, made from sulphuric acid, produces the same results without the danger. This is sodium bisulphate, sometimes called sodium acid sulphate. Dissolve a half-teaspoon in a few tablespoons of water, and you have a colourless solution with which to write secret messages. Heat the secret message and the letters will char while the paper stays white. Keep this chemical in a tightly stoppered bottle. It absorbs water from the air.

Dozens of other secret inks can be made using liquid, gas, or heat developers. Some of the best secret inks use none of these developers at all, but become visible under ultra-violet light. Such inks are said to *fluoresce*, and a number of fluorescent liquids can be used for writing. When held under a sunlamp or some other source of ultra-violet light, the message glows brilliantly. Under ordinary light the message cannot be seen. These inks are exciting and interesting. They are safe to use in experiments if you take the precautions that everyone should take with a sunlamp.

FLUORESCENT INK UNDER ULTRA-VIOLET LAMP

Never look at it directly without glasses. Put glasses on before you start the lamp going. Do not hold papers or chemicals under the lamp or expose your skin to it for more than a few seconds at a time. It is easy to get a bad sunburn from too long exposure.

Anyone who is really interested in secret writing can find many strange and unusual ways to conceal messages. The study will lead him into a knowledge of chemistry, heat, light, and various other radiations. This chapter and the last have dealt with only the simplest materials and methods, the kind that you can easily use and understand with just a bit of help. But help can go only so far, and this is far enough. From now on you are on your own with codes and secret writing. If you have practised and want to check the answers to the practice exercises, you will find them on pages 120–4. As I've said in code several times during the first chapter, I hope you enjoy 'Codes and Secret Writing'.

Suggested Sources for Chemicals Mentioned in
Chapter 8 and 9

Ammonia (ammonium hydroxide)
          Grocery store
Ammonium chloride
          Chemist, chemical supply house
Baking soda (sodium bicarbonate)
          Grocery store, chemist
Chloride of lime (calcium hypochlorite)
          Grocery store, ironmongers
Copper sulphate
          Chemist, seed store
Cobalt chloride
          Chemical supply house

Epsom salt (magnesium sulphate)
>Chemist

Iron sulphate (ferrous sulphate)
>Chemical supply house, chemist

Lead nitrate
>Chemical supply house

Phenolphthalein
>Chemist, chemical supply house

Salt (sodium chloride)
>Grocery store

Sodium iodide
>Chemist, chemical supply house

Sodium nitrate
>Chemist, chemical supply house

Sodium sulphide
>Chemical supply house

Sodium bisulphate
>Chemical supply house

Tincture of iodine
>Chemist

Washing soda (sodium carbonate)
>Grocery store

1. Remember that only a small amount of each chemical is needed – an ounce or so will be sufficient.

2. Make up a fresh solution each time and label each chemical and chemical solution so you are sure of what you are using.

3. Treat every chemical as if it were something dangerous even if you know otherwise. Keep them away from your eyes and mouth. Several of the chemicals listed are poisonous if you swallow them. All are safe if handled carefully.

Answers to Practice Exercises

Chapter 2, p 25

1. 2–5–3–1–18   5–6–21–12–20   8–5–18–15–25
   1–12–20–18–5   1–19–21–18–5
   18–9–19–25–15   21–18–5–14–5
   13–25–1–2–3

2. 6–15–12–12–15   23–8–9–13–3
   12–15–19–5–12   25–1–14–4–18
   5–16–15–18–20   23–8–1–20–8
   5–4–15–5–19   1–7–5–14–20
   20–23–15–10–1

3. 1–3–15–4–5   9–19–12–9–11   5–1–14–5–23
   12–1–14–7–21   1–7–5–25–15
   21–13–21–19–20   16–18–1–3–20
   9–19–5–9–6   25–15–21–23–1
   14–20–20–15–11   14–15–23–9–20

4. NO CLUB MEETING TOMORROW

5. CODE WORK REQUIRES CONSTANT PRAC-
   TICE

6. BE CAREFUL YOU ARE BEING FOLLOWED
   BY ENEMY AGENTS

Chapter 2, p 27

   SEND HELP

Chapter 2, p 30

4. WHEN YOU PUT IT INTO A PEN
5. WHEN IT IS MADE INTO A RULER
6. A JEWELLER SELLS WATCHES AND A JAILER WATCHES CELLS

Chapter 3, pp 32-3

[coded symbols]

[coded symbols]

[coded symbols]

4. I DON'T KNOW THE ANSWERS
5. ARE YOU GOING TO THE GAME ON FRIDAY
6. THIS CODE IS AN OLD STANDBY FOR SCHOOL BOYS

Chapter 3, pp 35-6

1.
2. } Answers may vary slightly depending on your
3.   spacing. Have a friend check your work.
4. THIS IS A POSITION CODE
5. KEEP THE ALPHABET STRIP ON THE MARGIN

Chapter 3, p 36

SEND HELP TONIGHT

Chapter 4, p 45

1. PAROA YIGKY GXAYK JIUJK YZUYK TJSKY YGMKY HGIQZ UXUSK

2. KYVJV DRGYF IVTFU VZJNZ UVCPL JVUZE
   KYVER MPRST

3. XLCNZ YTHSZ TYGPY EPOES PHTCP WPDDL
   WDZTY GPYEP OLYPI NPWWP YENZO
   PEZRZ HTEST ESKTX

4. CODE WHEELS WORK QUICKLY

5. ACCURACY IS ESSENTIAL IN DECODING

6. PRACTICE AND MORE PRACTICE MEANS
   SUCCESS WITH CODES

Chapter 4, p 52

1. ULXDE OFMLN MGFHX

2. OCNTE HRZDH SNWOS OZBEX

3. CRRBM WIAYG VEQWM VHRSY TTLKX

4. COME HOME QUICKLY

5. HELP THE CASTLE FALLS

6. THESE CODES ARE HARD TO BREAK

Chapter 5, p 56

1. EGRLA PEAAE PROCD SSELS WIEAC DAALN
   OWSNX ETNOE AWLAA RTRBD

2. AOFCA AEIAC PEWSE UATEO SIUIN AAOTD
   NFIIL MRCNI HRAST PSHCN TTTOW SDPEX

3. TENOA MESLD CPEEM SCNEE AEOED RNTEI
   IWRTV HUINR YAIYE IHRDO TOFDR TCDSU
   IGHCV LASUW

4. RAIL FENCE IS THE FASTEST TRANSPOSI-
   TION CODE

5. CODE MACHINES ENCIPHER AND DECIPHER
   MESSAGES RAPIDLY

6. THE STUDY OF THE HISTORY OF THE
   ALPHABET REVEALS MANY STRANGE FACTS

Chapter 5, p 60

1. BHSO RETL IPOD NLTO GAHA TNEK

2. TETSR RBEEE EUNAD ARPSR SIATO UECOC
   RDEFK
3. WATUR ESIBS APNHC REGOH ECIUO HINSO
   AATEL VLHAW IMEFX NECTY GELEZ
4. HAVE SMITH REPORT IN PARIS NOW
5. CONTACT AGENT B TWO AT ONCE
6. CONSTANT PRACTICE TRAINS YOU TO
   AVOID ERRORS

Chapter 5, pp 67–8

1. DPEOO LEMNA TEOCI TTENO CXGMY
2. EREWA NESIL CSRTL EPEHW ZAQCO ITUOR
   MIIDK
3. ATLOC LHEFO YEDBD SSCRE ICRES SIYAI
   TEPKS UNTIC VCANA WENGL
4. BLOOD WILL FLOW IN THE STREET
5. HELP WILL COME FROM MY FRIENDS
6. AFTER YOU LEARN TO MAKE CODES LEARN
   TO BREAK THEM

Chapter 6, pp 79–80

1. EVERYTHING THAT CAME HERE IS ON
   HAND ('B' code)
2. HAVE EACH AGENT TAKE NOTE OF THIS
   ('Z' code)
3. TABLES OF LETTERS ARE THE ONLY AID
   IN BREAKING CODES ('L' code)

Chapter 7, p 91

LISTEN MY CHILDREN AND YOU SHALL HEAR
OF THE MIDNIGHT RIDE OF PAUL REVERE

Chapter 7, p 93

1. IGPAY ATINLAY ISWAY HETAY EASIESTWAY

ANDWAY OSTMAY IDELYWAY USEDWAY
ECRETSAY ANGUAGELAY

2. AWAY ANMAY HOWAY ASHAY TUDIEDSAY
ECRETSAY ANGUAGESLAY AYSSAY HATTAY
IRLSGAY EARNLAY ANDWAY USEWAY
IGPAY ATINLAY UCHMAY EASIERWAY
ANDWAY OREMAY OFTENWAY HANTAY
OYSBAY

3. INWAY HETAY IDDLEMAY AGESWAY
ATINLAY ASWAY HETAY ANGUAGELAY
OFWAY CHOLARSSAY ANDWAY EARNEDLAY
EOPLEPAY. ITWAY ASWAY HETAY
ANGUAGELAY USEDWAY INWAY EACHING-
TAY ANDWAY INWAY HICHWAY OSTMAY
OOKSBAY EREWAY RITTENWAY

4. THE AVERAGE LENGTH OF WORDS IN THE
ENGLISH LANGUAGE IS ABOUT FOUR AND
A HALF LETTERS

5. IN ALL THE COMMON LANGUAGES OF
WESTERN EUROPE AND AMERICA E IS THE
LETTER THAT IS USED THE MOST OFTEN

6. WORDS LIKE ADDED, PASSES, ERROR, OR
SEEMED ARE NOT GOOD TO USE IN CODES
BECAUSE THE REPEATED LETTERS MAY
GIVE THE CLUE ON WHICH THE CODE
CAN BE BROKEN

Index

FREE

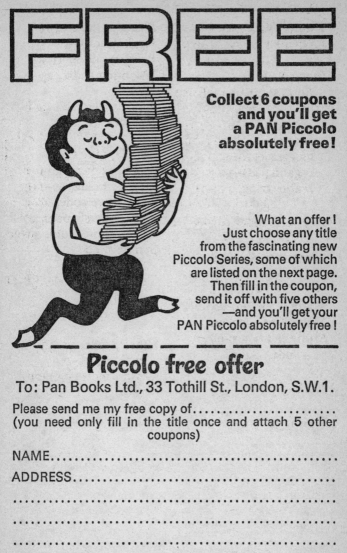

Collect 6 coupons and you'll get a PAN Piccolo absolutely free!

What an offer!
Just choose any title
from the fascinating new
Piccolo Series, some of which
are listed on the next page.
Then fill in the coupon,
send it off with five others
—and you'll get your
PAN Piccolo absolutely free!

Piccolo free offer

To: Pan Books Ltd., 33 Tothill St., London, S.W.1.

Please send me my free copy of........................
(you need only fill in the title once and attach 5 other coupons)

NAME...

ADDRESS...

....

....

....

This offer, which is available only in the U.K. and the Republic of Ireland, closes on December 31st, 1971.

Piccolo

THE OTTERS' TALE (illus., double format landscape)	Gavin Maxwell	25p
FUN-TASTIC (illus.)	Denys Parsons	20p
SEVENTH JUNIOR CROSSWORD BOOK	Robin Burgess	20p
SEVENTH JUNIOR PUZZLE BOOK	Norman G. Pulsford	20p
NUT-CRACKERS (illus.)	John Jaworski & Ian Stewart	20p
101 BEST CARD GAMES FOR CHILDREN (illus.) 	Alfred Sheinwold	20p
FUN AND GAMES OUTDOORS (illus.)	Jack Cox	20p
THE JUNGLE BOOK	Rudyard Kipling	20p
THE SECOND JUNGLE BOOK	Rudyard Kipling	20p
FIRST JUNIOR PUZZLE BOOK	Norman G. Pulsford	20p
FIFTH JUNIOR PUZZLE BOOK	Norman G. Pulsford	20p
SIXTH JUNIOR PUZZLE BOOK	Norman G. Pulsford	20p
FIRST JUNIOR CROSSWORD BOOK	Robin Burgess	20p
SECOND JUNIOR CROSSWORD BOOK	Robin Burgess	20p
FIFTH JUNIOR CROSSWORD BOOK	Robin Burgess	20p

TRUE ADVENTURES

PIRATES AND BUCCANEERS (illus.)	John Gilbert	20p
GREAT SEA MYSTERIES (illus.)	Richard Garrett	20p

COLOUR BOOKS
(Full colour illustrations throughout)

DINOSAURS	Jane Werner Watson	25p
SECRETS OF THE PAST	Eva Knox Evans	25p
SCIENCE AND US	Bertha Morris Parker	25p
INSIDE THE EARTH	Rose Wyler & Gerald Ames	25p
EXPLORING OTHER WORLDS 	Rose Wyler & Gerald Ames	25p
STORMS	Paul E. Lehr	25p
SNAKES AND OTHER REPTILES	George S. Fichter	25p
AIRBORNE ANIMALS	George S. Fichter	25p